TTY OF GOD

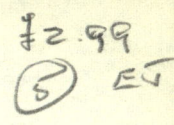

The Devil
and the
Sovereignty of God

Lynda Rose

KINGSWAY PUBLICATIONS
EASTBOURNE

Copyright © Lynda Rose 1995
The right of Lynda Rose to be identified as author if this work
has been asserted by her in accordance with the Copyright,
Designs and Patents Act 1988.

First published 1995

All rights reserved.
No part of this publication may be reproduced or
transmitted in any form or by any means, electronic
or mechanical, including photocopy, recording, or any
information storage and retrieval system, without
permission in writing from the publisher.

Unless otherwise indicated, biblical quotations are from
the New International Version © 1973, 1978, 1984
by the International Bible Society. Use is also made of the
New English Bible (NEB), © The Delegates of the Oxford
University Press and the Syndics of the Cambridge
University Press 1961, 1970.

ISBN 0 85476 289 2

Produced by Bookprint Creative Services
P.O. Box 827, BN21 3YJ, England, for
KINGSWAY PUBLICATIONS LTD
Lottbridge Drove, Eastbourne, E Sussex BN23 6NT.
Printed in Great Britain.

Contents

Foreword	9
Introduction	11
1. The Problem: Does Evil Exist?	20
2. What Is Temptation?	30
3. The Reality of Choice	43
4. Who Is the Devil?	78
5. Jesus and the Devil	107
6. The Devil's Strategy	122
7. Satan Exposed	142
8. The Devil and Hell	154
9. Angels	177
10. Demons	201
11. Curses	226
12. The Devil Today	247
13. Come Close to God	267
Epilogue	275
Scripture Index	277

*I would like to thank my family for their
love and support throughout the writing of this book,
and especially my husband, who has given tremendous
practical help, above all in the reading, correction
and final preparation of the manuscript.*

Foreword

This is what I term a 'well ticked' book.

Lingering sub-editing habits make me a hyperactive reader, addicted to underlining, circling and the judicial use of the asterisk.

A prized tick in the margin, however, is reserved for one of those disclosure moments of life; the ones that break out in a slow smile with an under-the-breath 'Wow!' If this is followed by a chuckle, a brace of ticks is awarded.

Lynda Rose's book—triple-ticked on occasions—well and truly puts the devil in his place and lifts the reader high to the rock which is Christ.

In doing so she avoids the pitfalls of many in this genre of Christian book. She takes Satan seriously, assigning him the required respect (Jude 9), but with fine biblical balance shows him to be a created being who exists and works firmly within God's purposes whether he likes it or not.

In a generation when many in the church smirk at the devil, in harmony with television adverts and comics, Lynda's logical, biblical and commonsense approach to her subject is timely, and more than welcome.

For too long, the devil has had his own way among the backward Christian soldiers who sit down for Jesus, and watch their fellow spiritual gladiators fight the good fight on their behalf.

Perhaps this book will recall many who have gone AWOL!

Kevin Logan

Introduction

I was talking at a Cambridge college on the practice of prayer. Towards the end I made the observation that, as soon as we resolve to spend more time alone with God, the devil will try to thwart or distract us, and that one of the ways to counter this was to be disciplined in our prayer life. Afterwards a group of students came up to me and said, 'That was fascinating, but you don't really believe all this stuff about a devil, do you?'

As a Christian I do believe in the existence and malignity of a personal devil, but I also recognise that these young people—intelligent, articulate, the world at their feet—are in no way exceptional in their attitude. This book is dedicated to all those for whom evil is a realm of utter confusion, and the idea of personality behind evil quite incomprehensible.

There is a very strange phenomenon abroad today. It has two aspects, both of which are extremely dangerous. The first view is a kind of sanitised belief, virtually unique to the Western world, that runs something along the lines of: 'God (whatever he is) is good. God has created a good world. He desires for us only what is good. Therefore, in spiritual terms, there is nothing bad. Bad things undeniably happen, but they are a product of man's mismanagement, basic greed, desire for power, et cetera, or simply a by-product of the unfortunate effects of nature. In itself, therefore, there is no such thing as evil, and certainly nothing so preposterous as a devil.'

Now this argument comes up against a stumbling block, because Jesus appears to have thought that there was a devil. Even worse, he seems to have operated under the misguided belief that the focus of his ministry was actually a struggle with this personage. But, according to exponents of this view, he cannot really have meant that, not if he was the Son of God and actually did know about such things. No, what he must have been doing was framing his teaching and ministry in terms that his first-century disciples would have understood. An even more extreme version of this position maintains that Jesus suffered from a first-century worldview, and so could only see his ministry in those kinds of limited terms himself. If he were to walk the earth again today, he would not be so naive. This way of thinking then happily dumps all the teaching of the Bible that it finds unacceptable.

The other view that holds such powerful sway today is almost the direct antithesis to this kind of thinking. Superficially it is straight down the line, Bible-based and wholly good. Jesus taught that there was a devil . . . and he was right. There is most certainly a DEVIL! In fact he's everywhere, and Christians are locked in unholy combat from the word go.

The trouble with this view is that it leads us to eternal conflict with a vengeance. The outcome is pretty close run and, though we know we have the final victory, for many of us it feels like we are suffering present defeat. Demons are everywhere, and they are very, very powerful. Everything that happens, happens because there is a demon around, whether it is stubbing your toe on the bed post when you leap out of bed in the morning, or suffering a major heart attack. Everything that produces the least feeling of pain or upset is of the devil. It has got to be, because God is good, and we are engaged in a spiritual battle!

I believe both these views are very, very dangerous. In fact, I would venture to suggest that both views come straight from the devil. Only consider: if the devil really is the powerful foe Scripture says he is, what better way of carrying on his campaign and creating absolute mayhem than creating in people's minds the illusion (a) that he doesn't exist or (b) that he is practically equal in power to God.

View (a) gives the devil a licence to do whatever he wants. But view (b) must delight him just as much. True, this view takes seriously scriptural teaching on the problem of evil, but it instils such a fear of overwhelming demonic power that it focuses the mind of the believer on the devil rather than on God. It destroys the child-like unquestioning trust in God that Jesus so strongly taught us to hold. Christ's victory on the cross becomes something that we ourselves have to re-enact. We have to win again that victory. On this line of thinking, we are soldiers of Christ—no doubt about it—but we are out there in no man's land, all by ourselves, and the devil is very much closer to us than God.

I have met many Christians who see demons everywhere, or who feel themselves to be battling against the overwhelming odds of some inherited curse, from which by themselves they are powerless to break free. I have seen Christians in near despair, in confusion and in terrible pain . . . because their gaze has been locked on the devil, when the answer was for them simply to come closer to God.

Many of the problems people experience today arise from their disobedience to God. The devil is not all-powerful. He does not have an unbreakable stranglehold on lives, unless he is permitted to do so. There is no magic—a quality which has sadly existed in some of the deliverance ministry I have seen in recent times. God alone is all-powerful. He *does* have the victory. Nothing in heaven or on earth can stand against the cross of Christ, and the answer for all our problems—whatever they might be—is simply to come closer to God.

Now I am not belittling the real ministry that is exercised in setting people free from oppression. In fact, further on in this book I have a lot to say on this subject, and for myself I can say that I do believe in the existence of the devil as a power of evil. But I believe too that some of the supposedly Christian ministry being exercised has more in common with New Age teaching than with Christ, and this is in itself the giving of allegiance to other gods so explicitly forbidden throughout the Bible. St Paul, in his parting words to the elders at Ephesus, warned: 'I know that after I leave, savage wolves will come in among you and will not spare the flock. Even from your own number men will arise and distort the truth in order to draw away disciples after them. So be on your guard!' (Acts 20:29–31a).

A healthy perception of spiritual realities, grounded in the lordship of Christ, is one thing. An unhealthy obsession with warfare is another. Yet at the same time we must guard against the other extreme. I have seen much Christian counselling that is so rooted in secular therapy and modern psychiatric techniques that it is wholly incapable of touching the deeper spiritual problems that lie underneath and are the cause of the problems being experienced. This kind of approach is like bandaging bedsores, but doing nothing to heal the skin; it condemns people unnecessarily to a bondage from which they are powerless to break free.

Over the years a large part of my own ministry has been with those who are spiritually damaged in some way. It has never been a ministry I have sought—indeed, for a long time I tried to resist it—but the trouble was, people kept coming and asking for help. And not only that: things kept happening in our own lives as a family, things that sometimes felt like they were trying to destroy us. These ranged from sudden serious illness, to vicious and hostile attack by others, for which rationally there seemed no cause. And yet at the same time God seemed to be doing the most extraordinary things and we had tremendous encouragement and support from others. Therefore, I was forced to try and understand things that really I would have preferred to know nothing about.

So I came to face this question of evil and the power of the devil. I read all the books on spiritual warfare I could find, but nothing actually explained why the problem existed in the first place. I knew there was a problem, because I could see it all around . . . and I could see God's power. But *why* was there this struggle? What was going on? What was the right theological position on all of this?

This book, then, is concerned with theology, but it also seeks to address the problem of how we recognise when the devil is at work, both in our own lives and in society at large. This world is undeniably a battleground and we are all subject to attack, both Christians and non-Christians alike. If we cannot recognise that attack for what it is when it is being launched against us, then there is no way we shall be able to deal with it.

By way of example, a young man in his early twenties was having a terrible problem grappling with pornography, though this was not the reason he came to see me. He said that he had lost all direction. He had lost his job, he had no family and over all he could see no meaning to his life. It was only as we talked that his problem with pornography gradually emerged. It had begun in early childhood, he said, and as we talked it became clear that he felt a deep anger and contempt for his parents. He had never realised that there was anything wrong with pornography. His friends were all 'into it', it had seemed to him perfectly acceptable, so he had never realised the harm it was doing him. Now I am not suggesting that this was the sole cause of this young man's problems, because it was not, but it had most definitely affected the way he saw both himself and others—especially women—and it was something of which he needed to repent and from which he needed to be set free in order to recover any kind of joy in life.

There are many things today which give the devil access into our lives, and we are weak because we can no longer recognise them. As a society we have lost sight of God, and that means we have also lost sight of evil—something that delights the devil because it gives him carte blanche to carry on his work undisturbed. Two examples illustrate the dangers.

The young girl who served me in the newsagents was wearing around her neck an inverted cross. No doubt she was wearing this as a fashion accessory, but what I am sure she did not realise is that a cross inverted in this way is a powerful symbol used in black magic to call on the devil.

There is a school of thought today that says that if you do not believe in something, then it does not matter, even if you find yourself involved in it in some way. Thus, for example, it does not matter if you are a Christian but practise yoga, because, provided you do not believe in the spiritual disciplines that underlie the exercises, then spiritually they can have no effect. I disagree with this. We are told in the Bible that if we take communion while in a wrong relationship with God, then we eat and drink judgement on ourselves, which may well manifest as sickness and ill-health (1 Corinthians 11:27–30; see also Chapter 12 below for a fuller discussion of this point). In just the same way then, I believe that wearing a Christian cross when we profess no belief is dishonouring to God and *will* have an effect. But even worse, I believe that to wear an inverted cross as a fashion accessory will open us up to harm. Satan is actually indifferent as to our reasons for wearing it —what interests him is that we do! If we are not under the lordship of Christ, then he will regard us as fair game for himself. He will feel we have issued an invitation, and he will be quick to accept.

This may sound rather far-fetched, but I saw the effect all too clearly illustrated in the case of another young girl—I'll call her Beth—who told me how, in her early teens, she had dedicated her little finger to a Chinese guardian spirit. A group of her friends, she said, had been messing around at school. Now I am the first to admit that this, on any reckoning, sounds ridiculous, but as we were praying with Beth her hand began suddenly to rise very slowly into the air, apparently being pulled up by the finger. It looked extremely odd, but Beth could do nothing to stop it. In the end it looked almost as if she was being dangled from the ceiling, so at this point we cut her off from this spirit in the name of Christ, and the hand dropped. She afterwards related how, at that point, she had felt something go.

This book, then, is an attempt to answer a perceived need. We must ground our experience in theology but, at the same time, avoid a dry academic approach and ensure our theology is relevant to the present day. We shall, therefore, examine the nature of evil, and explore the implications for our lives and faith. Over the course of the book we shall look at such questions as: Exactly who and what is the devil? Where does he come from? What is his power? How does he exercise that power? Do demons really exist and, if so, what is their relationship to angels? But, most importantly, we shall look at what has been achieved by Christ.

The first few chapters may seem rather heavily theological, but I make no apologies for this. They are important because they explain our understanding of Satan and his ways from the Bible. Also there is extensive investigation throughout into the beliefs and assumptions of the people of biblical times, found in non-canonical literature and Jewish myth. These traditions are vital because they provide the context for many of the (otherwise obscure) references in Scripture, and help us to understand more fully the underlying thought processes of the biblical writers. To know them then gives us a clearer understanding both of biblical revelation and of our own beliefs and assumptions today. The more fully we understand, the more completely shall we know the sovereignty of God and be enabled to stand in his power. And that means victory!

Throughout the book I have also given examples based upon the situations of various people who have come to me for ministry. When referring to others, for their protection the names have been changed and one or two minor details (for example, work situation) have been altered. I hope that this will be a book for both believers and non-believers alike, and that it will set the struggle between good and evil into its proper frame. I believe that as we grow in understanding, so we come to live more securely in Christ, and in the victory that *is* most assuredly ours. I hope then that this book will help you to grow closer to God.

1
The Problem—Does Evil Exist?

'Just because bad things sometimes happen, how can you deduce from that the presence of evil in the world?' This was a question put to me recently by someone having problems, not just with the idea of a devil, but of God too. And at one level you can see his point—just because an earthquake rocks China, killing hundreds of people, why should that imply the work of the devil? Equally, is it possible to say that the atom bomb falling on Hiroshima at the end of the last war, and scoring a direct hit on the only Christian community in the whole of Japan, necessarily implied some kind of demonic agency, given that the thing itself was wholly the product of human endeavour and intent? Why absolve people of responsibility for something that has been designed, created and used with full knowledge and purpose? Why too should it imply evil if someone gets lung cancer from smoking cigarettes?

It is important to address the question of the reality of evil, outside human volition, at the outset of this book. If we seriously doubt the presence and reality of evil, then it makes the secondary issue of an organising force behind evil, in the person of the devil, rather redundant. Similarly it locates both angels and demons firmly in the realm of myth; and if that is where they belong, despite whatever Scripture says to the contrary, who is not to say that that actually is where we should place God too?

It is not possible to 'prove' the existence of God. Many have tried down the centuries, but to my knowledge no one has yet succeeded. And when you think about it, that has got to be right, because God is so much bigger than we are, and we can only know about him what he himself chooses to reveal. Moses discovered this at the burning bush when he tried to get God to reveal his name: 'Moses said to God, "Suppose I go to the Israelites and say to them, 'The God of your fathers has sent me to you,' and they ask me, 'What is his name?' Then what shall I tell them?"' (Exodus 3:13).

A perfectly reasonable request, you might think. But it was not so reasonable because, to the ancient Hebrew mind, to know the name of a man was to hold power over him, to control him—to be able in fact to bend him to your will. This was the very basis of magic. Moses was trying to get a handle on God, and God was simply not going to go along with that game. 'I am who I am,' he answered—and if that is not a divine way of saying 'mind your own business', I don't know what is. It had to be enough for Moses that God had revealed himself, because there was no way a mere man could hold power over God.

Now 'proof' has something of the same quality or feel. If we can prove God, we can get a handle on him. We shall know him, we shall know the way he operates . . . and that carries with it the suggestion that somehow we can manipulate him; we can mould him to our will. If we could prove God, our minds would be able to embrace him, and we would therefore be bigger than him. As it is, we can know God only by his revelation, and the evidences of his love.

Now Satan is not of the same stature as God, and his workings do not have the same ineffability. But, just as we cannot definitively prove the operation of goodness, so we cannot prove its reverse—though I believe most people would agree that we can recognise it. People speak, for example, of the catastrophic effects of pollution on the environment as 'evil', or of the 'evils' of nuclear waste. We call Hitler's mass extermination of millions of people in the last war 'evil', and we condemn as evil the conditions that lead to starvation and sickness in Third World countries.

The list is endless and, taken together, would appear to suggest—given what many feel to be a slowly disintegrating cultural climate in the world at large—that there is perhaps something more than mere chance at work here. But perhaps stronger evidence of something rather more focused is afforded by a brief look at our own motivations and compulsions. Long ago, writing to the young church at Rome, St Paul said, 'I have the desire to do what is good, but I cannot carry it out. For what I do is not the good I want to do; no, the evil I do not want to do—this I keep on doing' (Romans 7:18-19). How many of us have discovered the truth of this when trying, by sheer force of will, to give up some habit that we have felt was binding us?

Some years ago I had a friend who had managed to win the battle against heroin addiction. He had not, however, won it in his own strength. I well remember him commenting one day that addicts, though they may manage to give up the drug to which they are addicted, are never really free of it. It remains in the system like a slumbering snake, he said, ready at any moment to strike out. There is always a vulnerability, always a pain. He himself had experienced this. He told me that he had come to know the Lord and given his life to Christ; but he had still known that he was caught by the stuff, and it was crippling his life. Then one day, he had been driving down the street and he had seen a church, with a great crowd of people pouring in. He said he had not known why, but he found himself stopping the car and joining them. As he went through the doors, he began to run. He ran straight up to the man who was speaking and literally threw himself at his feet. He hadn't a clue why he was doing this; he had just felt the Lord behind him, pushing him. And, he said, the man reached out his hand and prayed for him . . . and he felt the 'thing' go.

Now this kind of bondage and dramatic freeing will not be the experience of most of us. But all of us will recognise the force of something we don't want gripping us, and will know what a struggle it can be to stand out against that temptation, and how impossible it can seem to be. In the same way, past hurtful experiences can emotionally cripple us and damage our capacity to form normal relationships or live happy adult lives. A girl who has been sexually abused for instance may grow into an adult who knows perfectly well that what happened was not her fault, nor typical of all relationships, yet still she finds herself locked into a pattern of response that maims from the outset any kind of relationship with another human being. In fact it seems to pervert every kind of response or feeling of emotion that she has to other people. She might even find herself re-enacting and imposing that same pattern of abuse onto another, even her own child.

In the same way we can meet people—we might even

be those people—for whom everything seems to go wrong. There seems to be no reason for it, but nothing they touch seems to go right: their job is an endless cycle of failure and frustration; their personal relationships lurch from crisis to crisis; they are never well; their children, if they have any, seem to be an endless source of trouble and disappointment, hopelessly rebellious. In fact, everything that could possibly go wrong does, and yet there never seems to be any good cause. Now it is all very easy to say, 'Well, it's their own faults. They shouldn't be such idiots. They invite disaster.' But the point is, when someone is locked into this kind of destructive life pattern, left to their own devices, it can be a cycle from which they are wholly incapable of breaking free. And even with the kind of 'counselling' that enables them to avoid getting into the same kind of situation again, they may very well find—and feel—that without something more, their life is a complete mess.

So what is going on here? If we really are the free agents that we are supposed to be, why do we get so caught up and generally messed around by all these things that seem to float around both inside and outside our heads, confusing and bedevilling us, and generally paralysing us when it comes to making even the simplest of decisions? The examples cited above appear perhaps rather extreme, but the kind of influences we are looking at can and do operate at every level. Why can we not resist that cigarette? Why do we go on hurting the person we most love when we know we don't want to? Why do we do that thing which we know deep down to be wrong? And that does not just have to mean something such as deviant sexual practice, or shop-lifting. It can just as easily mean something as apparently 'harmless' as gossiping, or doing something that we've said we won't—like eating cream cakes! What is it that just seems to take a hold of us and compel us, so that we can't break free?

The extreme rationalist may well say that it is because we are weak, yet even the most iron-willed individual will have areas of his or her life that cause pain. Very strong-willed, rational people, for example, not infrequently appear emotionally cold, and this can lead to all kinds of problems in personal relationships, with partners or children feeling unable to understand or cope, so that relationships break down and there is pain all round. So, quite apart from what the Bible says, the presence and pervasive nature of so much suffering in the world, and in the lives of every single man and woman on earth, suggests that there is something more at work here than mere random chance.

Now this is rather a gloomy picture from which, at face value, it may appear there is absolutely no hope of redemption or escape. But actually that is not the case. And it is the power by which people's lives can be wholly transformed that again suggests to me that it is not simply chance that causes so much pain and, on occasion, real tragedy. On the contrary, I would suggest that there is real evidence here of some organising and destructive force at work and that the struggle within—whether envisaged as something temporary or constant—is *real*. That is not to say that every difficulty in life is of demonic origin. God, I believe, teaches his children, and without a doubt that sometimes involves the overcoming of obstacles and even, on occasion, divine rebuke. But, where we feel ourselves to be the victims of compulsions or destructive habits from which we cannot break free, or where everything just seems constantly to go wrong, although there is no apparent cause, then I would suggest that it is not fanciful to say there is something more at work here, and that it is appropriate then to find out what it is.

Does evil imply personality?

Even accepting evil, some people have difficulty with the idea of a motivating force or personality behind it. They may have no problem with the idea of God—because he is good—but somehow they baulk at the idea of something that might actively will, and work for, what is bad. Now there are many reasons for this kind of difficulty and some of them do deserve serious attention.

Some people, for example, argue that if you admit the possibility of there being a devil, you take away from people the need for personal responsibility. If the motivating force behind wrongful and destructive behaviour can be attributed to some external entity bringing irresistible pressure to bear on the individual, they argue, then that individual is no longer responsible for his or her actions. Demonic activity has led to diminished responsibility. But the individual, they say, does bear responsibility. We all have choice, and it is up to each one of us to exercise that choice in the way that is right before God.

Now of course this is absolutely right, and we do all bear responsibility for our own actions and, to a more limited extent, for the effects of those actions upon others; but I do not believe that is quite what we are talking about here. In the Old Testament the devil was commonly called the tempter, or accuser. Certainly he brought trials to bear upon people. Job's physical sufferings, for example, were a part of the satan's attack on him, to try to get him to curse God, thereby renouncing his faith (Job 1:11; 2:4–5), and so demonstrate that his piety actually sprang not from love for God, but rather love for self. Throughout those trials, however, though the sufferings Job endured sprang from an outside source, he retained absolute personal choice when it came to a decision whether or not to continue in his commitment to God. And though Job argued and moaned, and called God unjust, he actually never wavered in that love, and so he remained righteous.

Now it may justifiably be said that Job's sufferings have absolutely nothing to do with the kind of compulsive behaviour we were talking about earlier, but at some point all habits start with a moment of decision. Once a decision has been made, the destructive behavioural pattern that has been embarked upon becomes progressively harder to break; first, because it grows in power and, second, because the will grows weaker as the man or woman involved becomes more 'used' to succumbing. And it is sad, but true, that evil unfortunately spreads far more easily than good, as pointed out by the prophet Haggai in his cryptic warnings to the returned exiles:

> 'If a person carries consecrated meat in the fold of his garment, and that fold touches some bread or stew, some wine, oil or other food, does it become consecrated?'
>
> The priests answered, 'No.'
>
> Then Haggai said, 'If a person defiled by contact with a dead body touches one of these things, does it become defiled?'
>
> 'Yes,' the priests answered, 'it becomes defiled' (Haggai 2:12–13).

To believe in a devil working tirelessly to spread disruption and chaos is in no way to deprive men and women of the responsibility laid upon them by God. On the contrary, obedience to God and the right exercise of choice become extremely important when one takes seriously the idea of a spiritual battle being waged.

The second major objection people commonly have is that they simply do not like the idea of there being any kind of organising spiritual force committed to causing harm. Such an attitude, they believe, is bred of superstition, only one step removed from the kind of animistic beliefs that saw trees and stones as inhabited by spirits and supernatural beings—the kind of beliefs, in fact, that in the West we abandoned centuries ago. In the same way, they condemn as naive and detached from any kind of spiritual reality, the stereotyped picture of the devil as a cloven-hooved, horned figure with a forked tail, clutching a pitch-fork in his hand.

Now to argue in favour of there being a devil does not in any sense mean that one has to subscribe to this view, any more than it means that God has to be viewed as a benign old man with a flowing beard, sitting on a cloud. This kind of picture of the devil is in any case of comparatively recent origin. What it means is simply an acknowledgement that behind the evil present in the world is an organising force or entity that can and does possess focused direction—that being the opposition and overthrow of that which is good and springs from God.

There is one further, though rarely voiced, objection that needs to be looked at: plain fear. It has to be said that some Christians find the idea so scary that they would prefer simply not to consider it at all. In my teens we had a dog called Major, who had one overriding fear. He was absolutely terrified of thunderstorms. At the faintest hint of a rumble he would dash hell-for-leather upstairs and dive for cover under the nearest bed. Now he was a very large dog, and the beds were standard size, so the effect was that his head would be safely hidden, but his rump and the greater part of his body would still be protruding, uncovered, into the room. The storm would then crash and rage all around, but he cowered, safe in his little sanctuary, apparently convinced that nothing could touch him. If we resolutely refuse to acknowledge the existence of focused evil—that is, the devil—we are just like poor Major, cowering with our heads under the bed. But that does not affect the reality of the storm. And, though our heads are well and truly buried, our bodies are still out in the open; and merely refusing to acknowledge what is going on around us is not a very safe form of defence.

Of course, people are absolutely right in their desire not to focus on the devil—on any count that is an extremely dangerous thing to do. But to come to a right understanding before God of the operation and goals of evil is actually to begin to realise, in its fullness, the victory Christ has given to us by his death on the cross, and not only to become properly equipped, but to learn how to use the weapons God has entrusted to our care.

First, however, we need to understand how evil gains a hold over our lives, and for that we need to look at the operation of temptation.

2
What Is Temptation?

Although it comes as a surprise to many people, the Old Testament does not specifically say a great deal about the devil, but it does have a lot to say on the nature and function of temptation and the evil that arises from rebellion or disobedience to God's will. For the Old Testament writers, testing by God was an integral part of the human condition. God used it as a means of teaching and proving the faithfulness of mankind. The idea of an independent and powerful force hostile to God emerges clearly only later (see Chapter 6 below). This is not to say, however, that there are not disruptive and antithetical forces present, most clearly seen in the pagan gods to which the nations surrounding Israel offer worship. Yahweh, however, is sovereign—the God of gods—and these forces cannot touch the Children of Israel while they remain faithful to his will, and so under his protection. The Jews, in fact, become vulnerable only when Yahweh withdraws his protection as a consequence of their disobedience.

There are, then, important lessons for us to learn here. To begin with, God tests his children—and that will sometimes mean that we fail. But while nothing can happen without God's permission, suffering never originates with God (see James 1:13–14). We shall examine this in detail as we look at the workings and weapons of the devil in Chapter 4 below, but there are two points to be made here. The first is that much of what we call suffering—whether it is sickness, financial hardship, relationship problems, emotional stability or whatever—originates in our disobedience to God, and that is not dealt with by rebuking demons or renouncing the devil, but only by sincere repentance, by a conversion of our lives, and by a return to God.

Secondly, much apparent trial that is not rooted in sin (and, if you believe no trial happens without sin, just look at Jesus in the wilderness) is permitted for the testing and strengthening of our faith. It is caused by the devil, but it is God himself who has led us to that place, and who permits it. It is an inescapable part of our training if we are to serve the Lord. So let us look at the scriptural foundations for this.

Is temptation evil?

Sin, we are taught, originated in the Garden of Eden when first Eve, and then Adam succumbed to the temptation of the serpent. So many people get hung up on discussing whether or not the stories attaching to our creation and our disobedience are literally true, but I would ask you now to suspend that debate and consider simply the *meaning* behind the first few chapters of the Bible. Left to ourselves, we are separated from God by sin. We are not meant to live that way. We were created to live in and care for the world, enjoying an easy and direct relationship with God. But something happened to spoil that relationship. In the Genesis story we are not told how evil managed to worm its way into Eden.

Indeed as the narrative is framed, it does not seem to be anything out of the ordinary; it is simply there. But, whatever the cause, Adam and Eve did wrong in listening to the voice of temptation and choosing to disobey God, and that choice put a wall between them and God—something from which humanity now suffers universally.

Eden, we are told, was in itself a special place. It was a garden that God made in the east of his creation. It was different from the rest of the world. It was exceptionally beautiful, and within its bounds Adam and Eve would have wanted for absolutely nothing. But it had a built-in crunch spot—a danger zone that you might think should have been surrounded with barbed wire and warning signs—because in the middle of the garden God put two special trees: the tree of life and the tree of knowledge of good and evil.

Now for some unexplained reason Adam and Eve appear never to have got round to eating from the tree of life, although God only said that they were not to eat from the tree of knowledge. As the story is told, God did not forbid them to eat from this tree in order to keep them in a state of dependence and ignorance, but solely for their protection: '. . . the Lord God commanded the man, "You are free to eat from any tree in the garden; but you must not eat from the tree of the knowledge of good and evil, for when you eat of it you will surely die"' (Genesis 2:16–17).

It may be thought that if God had not wanted Adam and Eve to eat from this particular tree he would have been far better (a) not to have put the tree there in the first place, or (b) not to have told them about it. The point is, however, that it was never his intention to cocoon them from all possible avenues of harm. That would have been to have kept them as children or slaves, and God did not want that. Rather, what God wanted was for Adam and Eve to be able to exercise choice and so mature spiritually. To put it another way, he wanted their free obedience.

In the past it always struck me that God was not being entirely honest with Adam and Eve, and that at one level the serpent was entirely accurate when it told Eve that they would not die, but would simply know the difference between good and evil. I am older and wiser now, but this, I think, says something of fundamental importance about the nature of temptation. In physical terms Adam and Eve did not die, their bodies were not at that precise moment obliterated from the face of creation. And so often we do not see an immediate and direct consequence of sin, of choosing something we know to be wrong. Yet in fact it was the serpent who was deceiving them, and they *did* die, though it was not immediately obvious. They died spiritually. We shall look more closely at the agent of their death in Chapter 4. For here, the important point to note is that as a consequence of their free choice, Adam and Eve had separated themselves from God, and were no longer able to remain in the garden.

Evil then—that is, our own moral evil—originates in the will. The devil can tempt us. He can throw at us every weapon in his arsenal, whether it is sickness, or disaster, or financial ruin, or the loss of loved ones—all the things that happened to Job. But evil, for ourselves, arises when we give ear to the tempter and succumb. And God, who is a God of love—who loves us indeed as precious children—will respond to that wrong choice for the simple reason that he wants us back.

On this analysis, evil is anything that separates us

from God. It is the assertion and glorification of self in opposition to God. It is following self-will instead of God's will for us. Like Eve, it is saying, '*I* want to know . . . I want to manage for myself.' And once that fatal step had been taken, we see in the Bible the same pattern repeated over and over again . . . because from then on Adam and Eve found themselves out in the big wide world that was very definitely under the sway of the devil. It had become the spoiled realm of disobedience, and the devil had a handle on their lives—a handle from which they could not break free by themselves.

The history of the emerging Jewish nation contains endless tales of self-will and disobedience; of attempts by the people to provide for their own security. Over and over again we read of the people choosing self-reliance instead of reliance upon God. And so they bring down on themselves the wrath of God, because God expressly tells them that self-reliance is wrong—it is not what he wants. As he reveals himself to them, he shows them that he wants them to be a people for his own possession, and that means he is not going to share them. It takes some pretty stiff discipline at times to get them to understand that; for every step forward, they take a couple of steps back . . . and so the whole process starts over again.

The same is true for every one of us. When you think about it, we are a pretty stiff-necked species. We like to have our own way, and therein lies a seedbed in which the devil may cultivate all sorts of weeds. Evil originates in our putting self in the place of God—in making self our god. True, in Eden the temptation came from outside in the person of the serpent, but the actual evil arose when Eve succumbed to that seduction. Her problem was that she wanted to be equal to God. She wanted to know what he knew, and then she would not have to depend on him. That was the chance God took when he gave Adam and Eve free will. Temptation is a part of human existence, even prior to the Fall. However, evil only arises when the individual gives way to the enticement and acts upon it. What often comes as a surprise to people is that in the creation story there is actually at no point a parallel drawn between the serpent and the devil. In fact all the narrative says in Genesis is that 'the serpent was more crafty than any of the wild animals the Lord God had made' (Genesis 3:1). There is no hint as to why the serpent should wish to try and lead Eve astray in this way, while at the same time the beast is very clearly a part of God's creation.

We shall analyse the exact relationship of the serpent to the devil in Chapter 4, but at this point we need to recognise that men and women have implanted within them a strong desire for knowledge. That desire is not in itself bad, but the wrongful exercise of it can lead to a lot of problems. God wants us to be obedient to him, but that obedience only begins to have any real meaning once we have exercised choice. That is what testing is all about. It is coming into a real faith and learning to be obedient to God, not for what we can get out of it, but simply because we choose him! And that, of course, is why God gave us free will in the first place and, equally, why we are so vulnerable. God has created us as free spiritual beings. He wants us by the exercise of our wills to choose him: to choose the path of obedience. That choice will actually bring us real freedom and happiness, but he is not going to force us. To choose disobedience may appear to give us freedom, but actually it cripples us, because it makes us vulnerable to forces that are not of God.

What happened in Eden is a little bit like a couple of teenagers rebelling against the middle-class morality of their parents, and getting in with a gang which is definitely from the wrong side of the tracks! They start taking drugs and sleeping around, and then find that various members of the gang are pressuring them to become involved in petty crime. At first they try to resist, but the gang threatens them and, no longer able to return to their former lives, they are forced to succumb. The parents never wanted to restrict their children's freedom. In fact they only laid down limits because they knew that was the way that would provide for their best security and bring them happiness in life. The children, however, saw this as restraint, and so 'chose' something different—something that appeared to offer freedom, but which actually destroyed them.

This is the kind of scenario that we have underlying Eden, and we have all seen it repeated countless numbers of times as teenagers grow up! The trouble is, parents do not want to isolate their children from the world. We all want our children to be able freely to make the choices that will mean they can fend for themselves. But they can only get that way by making the decision for themselves. To prevent children from knowing what is going on in the big wide world is not going to achieve this. Yet of course, once having made the wrong choice, there is no going back.

So, once Adam and Eve had succumbed to temptation, they had to answer for their conduct before God. The serpent might have put the idea into their minds, but at no point is it suggested that they were not responsible for what they did. The temptation came from an external source. In itself it did not have any power. It gained power only when Eve listened and responded. But once that response was made, an irrevocable change took place, with the unfortunate result that Adam and Eve could no longer remain in Eden (the realm of obedience) and enjoy the free and direct relationship with God that they had up to that point. Sin produces separation from God.

The lesson for us here is that it is a part of the human condition that we shall always be subjected to temptation. In the same way, as Christians, we shall always be involved in conflict. We do not have any choice in the matter—but that does not mean that the two are necessarily the same. Indeed, it is only since the seventeenth century that temptation has been viewed as arising solely from evil, and as something designed to entrap and weaken. The biblical view of temptation is more accurately seen as something that puts to the test. This may be from the devil, in which case the intention is to spoil and destroy; but equally it may be something permitted by God in order to build up and strengthen. At no point in the Bible does temptation arise as something in separation from God. Where the satan appears in the Old Testament, he is an angel (renegade perhaps—we shall examine this later), but very clearly under the control of God. To put it another way, though his intent is hostile and he is obviously in rebellion, he cannot act beyond the limits of God's permission, as seen from Job. Although Satan is God's foe, he is also, therefore, in the Old Testament very definitely God's tool.

In recent times I have come more and more to appreciate those words in the Lord's Prayer: 'Lead us not into temptation, but deliver us from evil.' Before, the first part had been inexplicable to me because, as I saw it, it was the devil who was responsible for temptation. But now I understand that although the devil actually causes it, it is something ordained by God and is actually a part of his gift. Yet for all that, temptation can be very terrible, and there is no way that we can stand against it in our own strength; while, over and above that, unconfessed and unrepented sin gives to the devil a hold over us that God never intended, and can lead to much oppression and pain. Jesus understood better than any one of us the nature of temptation. We know that in his own life he was subjected to constant bombardment from the devil (see Hebrews 2:18), and we know too that there was real conflict that ended only in the final battle on the cross. But now I would go further and say that I believe he could not have fulfilled his role without that temptation—simply because he became fully man. I do not believe that he sailed through all the devil threw at him with Olympian calm. He never fell, true, but I believe that that would have made his temptations all the harder to bear because he would have had the full weight of the devil thrown at him—something to which we, thank God, are never exposed. Jesus was never subject to the devil's oppression because he never fell. When he placed himself under Satan's yoke in order to win our redemption on the cross, it was entirely of his own free will and an expression of his strength, not weakness.

The horror of Jesus in Gethsemane was the horror of seeing and coming under the yoke of the demonic—something we cannot even really begin to imagine. God's promise to us, however, is that while we hold to him, he will never allow us to be tempted without providing also the strength to endure and a way of escape (see 1 Corinthians 10:13). What I think that means is that God permits us to be tried in ways that will build up our faith, but he actually stands before us and shields us from the full venom of the evil one. However, because Jesus is the Son of God, he did not have that shield, and there is no way we can imagine the full pain and horror to which he was subjected. More than anyone else he understood exactly what it meant to beg the Father, 'Lead me not into temptation and deliver me from evil;' but he had the strength to go on, 'Yet not my will, but yours.'

Temptations have to come. It is only the yielding that is wrong. At the same time, we know that once yielded to, temptation becomes harder to resist in the future because sin, unfortunately, is like a disease that spreads unless firmly checked. And not only that, it needs the proper kind of medicine to get rid of it, because it will not heal left to itself. In fact, unrepented sin is like a wound in our sides through which the devil has unrestricted access. It has to be healed to stop that access, and the only way for that to be done is through Christ. This, however, is to anticipate the argument, and we shall come back to this point later.

Does God punish?

So what happens when we make a wrong choice? Biblical teaching is actually very clear. Someone said to me the other day that God does not punish because he loves us too much . . . which brings us straight back to the old chestnut that all pain or misfortune is of the devil and is therefore evil. Now I am not saying that a lot of pain and misfortune is not caused by the devil, but actually it is by no means the teaching of the Old or New Testament that God never punishes. On the contrary, there is every indication that from the beginning

God has not only taken the fact of sin very seriously, but he has also consistently acted in response. To say this, however, can raise problems, because people immediately begin to imagine God as some kind of implacable Judge Jefferys figure, condemning people to hell willy-nilly for sins they don't even know they've committed. That kind of view is very far from the truth, but again it is an issue that we need to look at in order to try to understand the workings of evil and get some kind of background to this personality we call the devil.

It is instructive here to look again at Eden, because once again we find that in the story of the creation and Fall, certain immutable truths have been revealed, not only about our own human condition, but also about the nature of God.

When God learned what had happened, his immediate response was to throw Adam and Eve out of the garden (Genesis 3:22–24). Now many people today find this difficult. After all, God had not really made it very easy for them, they argue. The least he could have done was to give them a second chance, when they might have had a clearer idea of what was involved. But this was not on. The trouble was, once they had made the choice, Adam and Eve could not go back to the state of innocence they had been in before. It is they who had changed the picture, not God.

If that is difficult to understand, think for a minute of a woman giving birth. Once she has had the baby, regardless of whether or not the child survives, her body has irrevocably changed. From that time on, even if she tries to keep the birth secret, any doctor who examines her will be able to tell. It is precisely this kind of change that took place in Adam and Eve—

something absolutely irreversible had happened. And it simply meant that they were no longer able to enjoy the same kind of relationship with God that they had enjoyed up to that time . . . because from that point on their own guilty knowledge stood before them, and it completely changed the way they looked at things (see Genesis 3:7). There was, however, more to it than that. They could no longer remain in Eden, not just because they were no longer fit to remain there, but because if they did, they might eat from the tree of life, and so live for ever in that state to which they had descended by their one rebellious act (Genesis 3:22).

At no point does their expulsion appear to be simply the outcome of anger. The picture of an enraged deity, mindlessly wreaking revenge or rejecting his creation in fury is markedly absent. On the contrary, there is every indication that what happened upset God profoundly, and even though he turned Adam and Eve out—in what almost seems an act of self-contradiction given the circumstances—he took the time to make them both some decent clothes. But even that is not the end of the story because once Adam and Eve were out there, painfully toiling and sweating as they tried to scratch a living, God watched over them and maintained contact with them . . . and he started to plan. We know he did, because we see the outcome of those plans in Christ.

The point is, this is not a God who does evil in return for evil, or who wantonly punishes simply from a desire to exact revenge. This is rather a God who responds in love to the evil choices made by others; but at the same time he is not some permissive parent who threatens and then never carries out the threat, no matter how bad the child. God's nature is such that he cannot and will not be other than he is. And he cannot and will not permit us to be less than he knows we can be. He will not permit us to stand in his presence while evil has a hold on our lives.

So God reacts, but this is by no means the complete story. Nor does it even begin to explain many of the situations, difficulties and disasters we all not infrequently encounter in life.

3
The Reality of Choice

In the last chapter we drew an analogy between temptation and the lures and trickery of a street gang. Satan is like the vicious leader of that same gang who despises our security and cosy lifestyle and tries, by whatever means possible, to lead us astray. God, our Father, does not want entirely to isolate us from his blandishments, or even his attacks, because he wants us to be 'streetwise'. He wants us to be able to stand on our own two feet and say, 'No!' But we have to face up to the fact that once made, our choices, whatever they are, produce an effect. Where we make a wrong choice, in the sense that we choose *for* evil and *against* God, then not only shall we open ourselves up to Satan's hold (we shall, in effect, take out membership of the gang), but we shall also trigger a response from God, and this might well be extremely uncomfortable!

As I see it, there are broadly five different scenarios that arise as a result of our succumbing to temptation. The first three have to do with the response of God to our wrong choices and actions and do not involve evil (that is, a force working in opposition to God). The fourth may be far more restrictively seen as having to do with God's training of the individual. The fifth and last is far more specifically concerned with the activities of the devil. It has to do with the situation where we, either by our own sin or the sins of others, have become opened up in some way to the demonic and are suffering as a result of that. This last is very important for our purposes, because the sufferings endured are sometimes wrongly attributed to God's punishment, or even mindless cruelty. Also, there is much confusion as to how, if this is right, such a situation can arise when God is omnipotent, and has allegedly won the victory!

This last scenario is perhaps what people today classify as the 'power encounter', and it is this area that the modern church is beginning increasingly to rediscover as it finds itself more and more faced with the demonic, the real evil. Let us, then, examine these different scenarios.

1. God's response to mankind's challenge

In the first situation we have our unbridled aspiration—the desire to challenge the position of God. Within the Old Testament, this is perhaps most clearly seen in the attempts of the first settlers to build Babel, the city with the tower that reaches to the heavens (Genesis 11:19). Interestingly, the plain where it was decided to build Babel eventually became the location for the city of Babylon—the city whose gods were seen to provide a constant challenge to the power of the one true God. With Babel we see the first attempt by men and women to break through the limits of their own humanity and to occupy the place that properly belongs to God.

While none of us likes to have our position usurped, this is especially true of God. In Genesis 11:5 we are told that God came down to see what was going on and was seriously concerned—because he knew only too well that if these arrogant builders succeeded in their attempt to challenge him, they would have broken through the constraints placed upon humanity and there would be no holding them. He knew that if they succeeded he would be redundant, and so he acted. His immediate response was to confuse their language. The result was devastating, far more devastating than if he had simply knocked down the tower, because in one fell swoop none of the people involved could understand each other, and so they could no longer co-operate together in order to carry out the project.

Now at one level this can of course be seen as retribution. God can perfectly well be viewed as having blasted them for their presumption. But this view is in conflict with the text: 'The Lord said, "If as one people speaking the same language they have begun to do this, then nothing they plan to do will be impossible for them. Come, let us go down and confuse their language so they will not understand each other"' (Genesis 11:6–7). This was not punishment, but rather God acting in order to prevent men and women from achieving autonomy in separation from himself. This was total rebellion, the raising up of another god (in this case, themselves) and God would not permit it.

Not so long ago, people everywhere were taking up the slogan 'God is dead!'. The underlying idea was that scientific advances had made God redundant, because we now possessed the powers to control and shape our own destiny. We had the ultimate weapon of destruction in the atom bomb, and the barriers of disease were rapidly breaking down before the advances of medicine. In just a few years, it was thought, we would have all the answers; we would have total control over sickness, we would be able to determine for ourselves the characteristics of our children, we would control our environment—we would in every sense become a race of super men and women. We are still following this argument, but it has not happened yet. The possession of terrifying weapons—whether atomic, biological or chemical—has in no way led to the elimination of conflict. Medical science has not succeeded in eradicating disease; indeed we are now faced with the plague of AIDS, while on all sides we seem to see an escalation of sickness, both physical and mental.

I am sure we have all heard it said—perhaps we have even said it ourselves—that present conditions are a part of God's judgement upon mankind's sin. Equally, I am sure we have come across others who have said, 'What utter rubbish!' But in the Bible God always acts where there is an attempt by men and women to rely entirely upon themselves, or on anything other than him. Each time there is this kind of turning away and self-glorification, we find that God responds, first by calling the people to repentance and a turning back (and sometimes in worldly terms God's commands seem utterly ludicrous) and then, if the people have failed to respond or have responded inadequately, to destruction of the thing relied upon (eg, Isaiah 3:16–26; 22:8–25). This is in no way to say that science or possessions, nor even power, are evil in themselves. Evil comes when we place our trust in these things, and when we exalt them, and claim for ourselves the position of God.

Neither is this kind of reaction on the part of God confined to the Old Testament. In the book of Acts, where Herod rather spectacularly addresses the people and they respond, 'This is the voice of a god, not of a man' (Acts 12:21–32), the response on the part of the Lord is instantaneous. We read that immediately an angel of the Lord struck Herod, because he too did not give praise to God, 'and he was eaten by worms and died'. In the same way Elymas the Jewish sorcerer (Acts 13:7–11) also falls victim to God's wrath when he tries to prevent Sergius Paulus, the proconsul of Cyprus, from hearing the gospel. Here he is trying to stop someone else from coming to a right perception of God, while at the same time retaining power by use of his magical arts. He is denying God his rightful position, and Elymas' punishment is to be struck with blindness, paralleling the spiritual blindness in which he has worked to keep others. So in the Bible we see that God punishes where men and women try to arrogate to themselves the position that rightfully belongs to him.

Some friends of mine recently moved house and were congratulating themselves on how well they had managed everything—particularly their finances. Within a month they had a car accident, not visibly very serious, and no one was hurt, but it cost several hundred pounds for the damage to be put right and completely wiped out their financial reserve. As we were reflecting on the incident some time later one of my friends said, 'You know, what this has actually done is force us back onto total reliance on God. We thought we were doing so well, but we were leaving God out of the picture. It just feels like he has brought us back on himself!' He had.

2. God's response to disobedience

A different situation arises where men and women actively disobey God's express commands. After the expulsion from Eden, it is almost immediately clear that men and women are from that point on under the influence of some malign force that consistently works in direct opposition to the way God wants them to live. For example, not only does Cain murder his brother, but from then on we see people falling prey to sexual licence and general debauchery, while the most horrendous practices are apparently accepted as the norm (eg, Genesis 6:5; 19:4–9). God, we know, destroys first the earth and then Sodom because of what is going on. The point is, from that moment of separation when Adam and Eve are turned out of the garden, men and women on their own have no defence against the manipulation of this evil force. And this force exercises its control precisely through those weapons of violence, greed, sexual immorality and perversion . . . all the things in fact that humiliate and destroy mankind and drive us even further from God. It is no accident that the cults that proliferated in the ancient world, such as those attaching to Ashtoreth and Moloch, incorporated into their worship sacred prostitution (of both a heterosexual and homosexual kind) and human sacrifice—sometimes of both adults and children. In the midst of all this God, we are told, marked out the Israelites as a people for his own possession—indeed the only people for his own possession, because through them he intended to implement a plan for the salvation of the whole of mankind. And so he began to teach them, revealing himself first to the patriarchs as a kind of clan God, and then through the exodus as God Almighty, the Creator and ruler of all things.

As he revealed himself, God laid down conditions for his worship. Those conditions were designed to ensure, first, that the people got to know him and honoured him in the way they should and, second, that they kept themselves free from contamination with other peoples. The principle was very simple. While the Jews obeyed, God would protect them against all opposition and would give them success in whatever they turned their hand to. When they disobeyed, he would withdraw that protection.

The Jews were never a large nation. When they first went into the Promised Land they found it peopled by all sorts of different tribes—the Canaanites, the Amorites, the Hittites, the Perizzites, the Hivites and the Jebusites. Against them the Jews were nothing. But, while they were faithful, God delivered all who opposed them into their hands. Jericho, for example, was initially taken not by armed combat, but by having the armed men march round the city behind the ark once a day for seven days, after which time all the people gave a loud shout, and the walls fell down (Joshua 6). There are many tales of miraculous success of this kind. While they obeyed, God watched over them and blessed them, but if they disobeyed, it was a very different story—because disobedience resulted either in God's withdrawal of his protection, or in his direct punishment.

As Moses warned the Children of Israel: 'If you ever forget the Lord your God and follow other gods and worship and bow down to them, I testify against you today that you will surely be destroyed. Like the nations the Lord destroyed before you, so you will be destroyed for not obeying the Lord your God.' (Deuteronomy 8:19–20). So, for example, we see the Israelites struck with plague after indulging in sexual immorality with the Moabite women, after having been expressly forbidden by God to enter into any kind of relationship with them (Numbers 25:1–9). And in the same way, as they begin the conquest of the Promised Land, we see the Israelite army suffer military defeat at Ai, although 3,000 of them turn out against only a handful of men. This time, however, it is not general disobedience that is the cause, but the sin of one man. Achan, in deliberate violation of the Lord's command after the capture and destruction of Jericho, keeps back some of the devoted objects plundered from the city. This, we read, 'is why the Israelites cannot stand against their enemies; they turn their backs and run because they have been made liable to destruction'. And so God warns, 'I will not be with you any more unless you destroy whatever among you is devoted to destruction' (Joshua 7:12).

At one level here God's reaction seems entirely disproportionate to the crime. It feels a little bit like one country cancelling a defence contract with another because one of the junior clerks has been pilfering paper clips. But it serves to show not only the weight God attaches to obedience but also, in God's estimation, the potentially powerful and dangerous effects of sin. Achan's sin could not be overlooked, not just because he had not taken any notice of what God had commanded, but also because he had brought contaminated objects in among the people and, left undisturbed, they would have spread a kind of spiritual and moral contagion that would have undermined and ultimately destroyed the autonomy of the Jewish nation. The sin had to be exposed and these objects had to be cleared out in order to cancel their effect and restore God's blessing.

If this reads like an extreme interpretation, it is worth considering that when on other occasions Israel disobeyed the Lord, whether it was to exterminate the general populace as they consolidated their hold on the land or to destroy shrines devoted to Baal, they stored up for themselves endless problems. On the one hand this was because the presence of the 'enemy within' led constantly to moral and religious decay, and was something the prophets had constantly to battle with as symptomatic of Israel's unfaithfulness to the Lord. On the other hand it was because as their sin intensified and grew (as it inevitably did), so it provoked God's wrath against them, to the extent that in the end their nation was almost entirely wiped out and the few who remained were sent into exile in Babylon.

This says something very important to us today, because the principle of obedience is still the same. If we are suffering untold problems in life and everything seems to be going against us, we would do well in the first instance to ask ourselves if there is any way in which we have been disobedient to the Lord. Now the answer might well be that we simply do not know. Joshua, the leader of the Jewish people, did not have a clue about Achan's sin and so he had to go to the Lord and ask him what was wrong. He did not receive an instantaneous answer; instead he had to remain face down on the ground the entire day begging the Lord to reveal to them why he had let this appalling defeat happen to them. It may be that we have to wait on God to ask him to reveal what has been wrong in our lives and then, when he shows us, to act on that. God's blessing is given to us when we live in obedience. He withdraws his protection if we are disobedient. The evil does not lie in the pain we experience, but in the wrong that is the cause. We are exposed to the difficulties and pain of evil because God will no longer shield or bless us while the things of the enemy have a hold on our lives. However, when we are obedient, it is a very different story:

> If you follow my decrees and are careful to obey my commands, I will send you rain in its season, and the ground will yield its crops and the trees of the field their fruit. Your threshing will continue until grape harvest and the grape harvest will continue until planting, and you will eat all the food you want and live in safety in your land.
>
> I will grant peace in the land, and you will lie down and no-one will make you afraid. I will remove savage beasts from the land, and the sword will not pass through your country. You will pursue your enemies, and they will fall by the sword before you. Five of you will chase a hundred, and a hundred of you will chase ten thousand, and your enemies will fall by the sword before you.
>
> I will look on you with favour and make you fruitful and increase your numbers, and I will keep my covenant with you (Leviticus 26:3–9).

However, where there is disobedience, God does not always respond simply by the withdrawal of protection. A different and rather horrific scenario develops where, as the result of sin, God then actively allows the wrongdoer to sink further into error and confusion. This is a strange situation. It appears, for example, to be the principle underlying Saul's descent into manic depression. Saul, the king chosen for Israel by God himself, seems to get it wrong almost from the word go. I have, I must confess, always felt a deep pity for Saul, because he seems to have been one of those characters who had everything going for him, yet for all his talents he could not cope with the position into which he was thrust. Part of my sympathy for him is that he had no role model to follow and clearly did not really know what was expected of him as God's chosen.

Consequently he tried to be a king like all the other kings round about—to make Israel militarily strong and a power to be reckoned with—but he left God out of the picture. This was not what God wanted at all, so his response was first to withdraw his spirit (his protection) from Saul and, second, actively to precipitate his downfall.

Nowhere do we see this more clearly than in the king's relations with David, the friend of his son, Jonathan. Saul at first loves David like a second son, but as David becomes increasingly successful in battle, that love turns to jealousy. Saul is wrong in that first instance to give way to temptation, but worse is to follow. We read: 'The next day an evil spirit *from God* came forcefully upon Saul. He was prophesying in his house, while David was playing the harp, as he usually did. Saul had a spear in his hand and he hurled it, saying to himself, "I'll pin David to the wall"' (1 Samuel 18:10–12, italics mine).

The straight reading of this is that this temptation, which is undeniably both evil and compelling, has been sent from God as a result of his displeasure with Saul. The choice of course still remains with Saul as to whether or not to respond. Whatever he felt about David, he could still have said, 'This impulse is evil. I will not do it.' But the point is that he no longer possesses the will for good and, as a result, God has not simply given him up to the consequences of his sin, but has actually ordained a situation of temptation in which the king, unless he turns and repents, will become far more deeply bound. This is exactly the situation painted by Paul in his letter to the Romans (Romans 1:24–32). Men and women deliberately choose what is evil instead of what is of God and so he abandons them to the consequences of their sin—to the extent of withdrawing his protection from their minds so that, by themselves, they are no longer capable of perceiving what is right.

This appears harsh, but it may be explained perhaps by the fact that it is total rebellion. It is the deliberate rejection of all God has said. It is the conscious glorification and indulgence of self, but to such a degree that there is no longer any room in the picture for God. Saul's first decisions and acts of rebellion were his own free choice. He was held in God's love, and he had been anointed with the Spirit of the Lord to guide him (1 Samuel 10). However, he chose repeatedly to act in disobedience, and it was that that provoked the Lord's wrath. The initial temptation arose in Saul's own mind. This was then exacerbated by evil coming from an external source. The point is that Saul had opened himself up to this evil as a result of his initial rebellion and sin. This happens for all of us when we consciously choose what is wrong: we become opened up to the devil in a way that completely exposes us to his attack. It is this opening up that has to be closed by repentance of the initial sin, and that can be accomplished only by Christ. But here in the case of Saul, the point has to be made that the evil impulse that grabbed him was not some renegade attack on the part of Satan, trying to undermine God's chosen one, but was an evil spirit absolutely under the control of God. There is never any suggestion of there being some force in opposition to God. What happened has in fact rather the quality of judgement. Where this kind of situation arises in our own lives, or the lives of others close to us, it is met only by sincere and absolute repentance, and a total conversion of life.

Odd as it may appear, this is very relevant for us today. In the Bible, God has laid down certain ways in which he is to be honoured. For example, the fourth commandment says: 'Remember the Sabbath day by keeping it holy. Six days you shall labour and do all your work, but the seventh day is a Sabbath to the Lord your God. On it you shall not do any work' (Exodus 20:8–10).

Now Jesus said that this commandment was constructed primarily for the benefit of men and women, and that we should not be legalistic in our application of it (Luke 6:5). Yet despite what many of us would apparently like to believe, this does not wholly negate the underlying principle of reverence shown to God by our observance. As a society today we are increasingly coming to flout this commandment (and Sunday Trading laws are only an example of the general attitude). At the same time, it is undeniable that society is becoming both increasingly morally decadent and violent, while on all sides many men and women are demonstrably unable to cope on their own. I genuinely believe that a part of what we are seeing here is the Lord's response to the turning of men and women away from him.

3. The hand of God

This situation is rather more difficult to understand, and is hard even to classify. To give an example from the Bible, when David became king of Israel he took the decision, having conferred with the people, to bring back the ark to Jerusalem. Some twenty years before, the ark had been captured by the Philistines, having been carried by the Israelites into battle as a kind of talisman. The Philistines, somewhat unwisely, had then placed it as a trophy in one of their own temples dedicated to the god Dagon. Disaster, however, had followed this move. First the statue of their god had been toppled onto its face, breaking it in pieces, and then, when they had decided to move the ark to more neutral ground, plague had struck (2 Samuel 5–6).

This, not surprisingly, gave to the Philistines a healthy respect for the God of the Israelites and, before further disaster struck, they decided to return the ark. Accordingly they put it on a cart, hitched it up to a couple of cows, and left it for the Lord to take it wherever he willed. The place he willed, as it turned out, was Beth Shemesh in Israel. It did not, however, stop there very long because, when seventy of the villagers died after having looked inside, they asked the people of Kiriath Jearim to take it off their hands. And there it stayed, until David decided to bring it home.

Now it may be thought that such a laudable decision, entirely in line with the Lord's commands, would bring only the most marvellous blessing. Such an enterprise, one would think, could not go wrong. Certainly that appears to have been what David thought. He gathered together a huge crowd, and with the most incredible celebrations, they all went down to collect the ark (2 Samuel 6:1ff.). They had made their preparations well. They had a cart, and two men, Uzzah and Ahio, were given the task of making sure it did not fall off. All went well until they reached Kidon, at which point the oxen pulling the cart stumbled, and there was every danger the ark would end up on the ground. This of course was absolutely unthinkable, and with commendable speed, not to mention presence of mind, Uzzah reached out and grabbed it. And what did God do?

THE REALITY OF CHOICE 57

The moment Uzzah reached out his hand, the Lord struck him down in anger, so that he died.

David was angry with God because, as he saw it, they had done nothing to merit the Almighty's wrath. But he did not only feel anger. From then on he was also afraid, so instead of completing their journey and returning the ark to Jerusalem, they turned aside and left it at the house of Obed-Edom, the Gittite. One can sense David's bewilderment at this totally unexpected turn of events, but let us consider for a minute what had happened.

Before the Israelites had entered the Promised Land, when God was welding them into his own people, he had commanded:

> ... appoint the Levites to be in charge of the tabernacle of the Testimony—over all its furnishings and everything belonging to it. They are to carry the tabernacle and all its furnishings; they are to take care of it and encamp round it. Whenever the tabernacle is to move, the Levites are to take it down, and whenever the tabernacle is to be set up, the Levites shall do it. Anyone else who goes near it shall be put to death (Numbers 1:50–51).

Now David was entirely right in his desire to bring the ark to Jerusalem; it was what the Lord wanted. But in his zeal David had entirely ignored these instructions the Lord had given so long before. To the Israelites the ark was literally the seat of God, invisibly present among them, but David had treated it simply as an object. He was over-familiar, lacking in all proper respect—and it was this disobedience that the Lord was reacting against. It was because of this that Uzzah died.

At no point do we hear of any Levites being included

in the triumphal band. Apparently they did not take part in, or even oversee, any of the preparations, and in direct contravention of all the regulations the Lord had laid down for transportation of the ark, it was not carried, but instead dumped on a cart. On top of all of this, the Lord had placed an absolute prohibition on anyone, for whatever reason, touching this symbol of his election and presence . . . but Uzzah did. The Lord could not allow himself to be dishonoured in this way, and so he struck out.

The overriding, if apparently harsh lesson here is that the Lord demands absolute obedience in everything he commands. It is not even an excuse to argue that 'no offence is meant'. However, it needs to be emphasised that the problem, as it is presented, is not disobedience to the Law, but rather a lack of honour and true reverence for the Lord, because that is what disobedience is.

Less surprisingly, God responds in similar fashion where there is a deliberate sin that dishonours him. For example, Ananias and Sapphira were both struck down dead after having lied to Peter about the price of a piece of property they had sold. They claimed that they were giving the whole sum to the Christian community, when in reality they were keeping back a part of the money for themselves. Peter defined this as a lie to the Holy Spirit, and accused the couple of having agreed with Satan 'to test' the Holy Spirit (Acts 5:1–10). The evil here lay in the couple having given way to the temptation of the devil, and in a way it was the same temptation that was held before Eve: 'Has the Lord really asked you to give all this money? Surely he wouldn't be so unreasonable! He won't know anyway if you keep some back . . . nothing will happen.' The enormity of their sin lay in the fact that when they gave way, they were dishonouring God—by putting him to the test of whether or not he would notice, or even care. This again begs the question: Does truth matter? It is that that God responds to. Again, it is simply not true that God never causes harm. There is no suggestion here that the deaths of the couple were in any way caused by the devil. Indeed the devil would appear to have had every interest in keeping them alive, because if they could have got away with the deception, there would have been no end to the harm they could have caused in the future among their fellow Christians; no end to the seeds of doubt they could have sown. The evil was in the sin; the consequence was wholly the response of God.

4. God's combat training

Not all suffering is either the result of evil (in the sense that it is caused by the devil) or a sign of God's displeasure. Some has in fact more to do with God's training or preparation for some greater task, without which the individual concerned would have neither the strength nor the resources. I believe that in this situation an analysis of what is going on is actually rather complex, and we shall return to this area at different points in the book in order to build up a fuller picture.

There are some people who even on casual acquaintance give every impression of having a hard time in life. You may even be such a person yourself. They are the kind of people for whom everything seems to go wrong—and even when things are going well, disaster just seems to hop up suddenly over the horizon and clobber them, good and hard. They are the kind of people who say, 'Why does it always happen to me?'

And sadly they are often Christians, who seem in every respect to be leading an exemplary life.

Now there are two possible scenarios here. One is quite definitely the outcome of some evil at work and should not be happening. But the other, though it will involve the workings of evil, has rather to do with what I call 'combat training'. It is closely allied to the temptations permitted by God for the deepening of our faith (see above, Chapter 2), but I believe that it differs significantly in degree—and, as you read this, you may well recognise some of the things going on.

So often I come across people who say, 'You know, since I became a Christian, life has been absolutely awful! Everything's going wrong. I seem to be under constant attack.' And sometimes they begin to ask about ancestral curses and oppression. Now it may be that they *are* under some curse, either as a result of something they themselves have done, or as a result of something done by past members of their family; but equally that may not be the situation at all. One possible reason is that what they are experiencing may simply be straight demonic attack, because there is nothing the devil loathes more than people who are committed to Christ. We must, however, recognise in this respect that nothing can happen to us without the express permission of God, as witness Jesus' words when before Pilate: 'You would have no power over me if it were not given to you from above' (John 19:11).

This whole area is not, I believe, very easy to grasp—at least, it has not proved so to me! As we come closer to God, he himself refines and purifies us, and strips away from us everything on which we rely that is other than himself. At the same time—and this, though it may not be very easily understood, is different—he skims away the dross from our lives, just as in making jam one brings all the ingredients to the boil, and then skims away the impurities as they rise up to the surface. What this means is that where there is then any wrong in our lives, at the right time God allows that to come to the fore, so that it can be removed. In this situation, I believe that God stands back and allows the devil to play havoc with us, in order to expose the hidden access point that the devil has to our lives.

This then is one situation, but there is also another, where God allows the most terrible trials, but which actually have nothing to do with any hold the devil has over us.

The devil constantly tries to attack us when we are committed to Christ. He does not bother if we are not, because there is no point. He himself will happily shower us with all sorts of goodies so long as we don't cast an eye in the direction of God; but let us once dare to do that and, quite literally, it can feel as if all hell has broken loose. Now Christ, once we come into a real relationship with him, shields us—that is a part of what the cross is all about—but I believe that sometimes he withdraws his protection so that we might learn. It is a little bit like letting a child walk by himself when he is just beginning to be steady on his feet. God is never very far away, but I believe he wants us to learn to use, under his authority, the gifts he has given to us.

When I began writing this book I was taken ill and I was extremely angry with God that he had allowed this to happen to me. I was also quite frightened because a lot of things had suddenly become extremely difficult. In fact, without God's intervention, they seemed impossible. One day as I was praying, or rather raging at him, he showed me a series of pictures. The first was a picture of myself in a long white dress. It was very new and very clean looking. I felt Jesus saying to me, 'You're wearing my dress. I've made it for you.' Then the picture changed, and he himself came and stood in front of me. He was absolutely huge and I saw that he was dressed in grey; in rags in fact. This time I felt him saying that he was wearing the clothes that had once been mine, and suddenly beyond him I saw the devil, throwing at him absolutely every demonic weapon he had. I understood that these were the things that should have been thrown at me; they were access points because of my old clothes. Now, however, they were all thrown at Jesus, and nothing at all could come near me. What I felt him saying was that this was the cross, and the devil could not touch me because of that . . . because Jesus stood there and he carried anything and everything the devil might have against me. From that point on, I believe he began to teach me that what I was suffering was demonic *temptation*, and that for some reason it had to be because of the work to which he had called me: he was fashioning me into something, forging something—and that something was new.

I am not trying to make myself out to be anything special—I know that I am not—but I relate this because I believe it is quite definitely one of the ways in which the Lord prepares us. I have heard people define it as a call to suffering, or as being allowed to share in the sufferings of Christ. I do not believe that is at all what is going on here, but at certain periods of our lives the Lord sometimes allows this so that we might be prepared for some purpose he has for us; and that purpose in the eyes of the world will not necessarily appear very great, but it will be God's purpose, and it will be important in the battle which is taking place in this world, and in the building up of his kingdom.

One character from the Bible who stands out clearly as having undergone the kind of preparation I am talking about here is Joseph. Joseph was the youngest son of Jacob. By all accounts he was thoroughly spoiled, being his father's favourite, and in his early years he comes over as rather a loathsome little toad, lording it over his brothers, and provoking their intense dislike. But the Lord had a purpose for Joseph. He had decided that Joseph was going to rise to a position of prominence in Egypt, second only to Pharaoh, and in that way would not only be the saviour of his people, but would also play a key role in preparing the Israelites for the place they were to occupy in history as the Lord's chosen people.

On any reckoning, Joseph appears to have been pretty unpromising material (see Genesis 37:2–11) and the Lord had his work cut out, not only in getting Joseph to the right place, but also in bringing him to a right attitude of mind for such a major task. The way he chose appears a bit rough. First, Joseph found himself beaten up and stripped by his brothers and flung down a well (Genesis 37:23f.). Then he found himself sold into slavery and transported to Egypt. Once there he found himself sold to Potiphar, Pharaoh's captain of the guard, and for a while at least it must have looked as though his luck was at last beginning to turn. The Lord gave him success in everything he did (Genesis 39:3). However, just as he must have been congratulating himself, disaster struck again. Potiphar's wife took a fancy to this personable young Israelite, and when he rejected her advances, she told everyone he had tried to seduce her. The result was that he was thrown into prison by her enraged husband (vv.13–20).

Yet again we learn that despite what had happened, the Lord was with Joseph (v.21). This particular point is actually important, because where hardship is a part of the Lord's training, at the same time there is very real blessing. This, then, is a major indicator in distinguishing between suffering allowed by the Lord for the purposes of preparation, and suffering that comes as a result of demonic hold. In the former, despite the pain (which can be very intense), there is real joy and a sense of rightness, while in the latter there is a strong sense of heaviness and oppression.

Here Joseph's trials were not over. The story goes on that while in prison (interpretation being one of Joseph's gifts), God used him to interpret the disturbing dreams of Pharaoh's chief cupbearer and chief baker, who had both ended up there having displeased their royal master. The cupbearer was released, protesting his thanks to Joseph and making promises of help . . . and promptly forgot about him. It was in fact a further two years before Joseph finally won his freedom, and then only when Pharaoh himself had a dream that no one could interpret—which served to prod the cupbearer's memory.

From that point on Joseph's rise was swift, but it had been a long and gruelling road for him to get there, and there must surely have been times when he bemoaned his fate, and asked himself what he could possibly have done to deserve all this trouble. Yet during those long, bitter years, God was forging in him qualities that would enable him to fulfil his role and give him the strength and toughness he was going to need if he was to survive.

In the Old Testament all evil spirits or demons, just as the angels, are seen as very firmly under the control of God. We can thus assume that in some convoluted fashion, it would have been axiomatic to the ancient mind that it was God himself who first put it into the minds of the brothers to murder Joseph. But the point to be made is that Joseph's sufferings—which must have been very real—were at no time seen as the result of evil at work in *his* life, nor was there any element of punishment in what he underwent.

One is reminded of some of the great saints who seem to have had to endure so much pain and general hardship. I have frequently heard it said that despite their apparent piety, what they went through must have been the result of some great evil in their lives that had given the devil a hold over them. But I simply do not believe this. Suffering does come as the result of demonic hold over our lives, but that is not the sole cause of pain. Some hardship is the result of evil's opposition to the outworkings of God's will (to put it another way: attack). And some is the result of God's preparation, when he withdraws his protection for a while so that we might learn.

Discernment is needed to understand the cause of whatever it is we are going through, and it is very important because if we attribute suffering to the wrong cause, then we take the wrong action. If we do this, at worst the result is absolute disaster; at best, nothing happens at all.

I believe that in recent years the church has been rediscovering an enormous amount about God's power, and the very real battle that is going on. But I believe too that that has led some to focus on the demonic in a way that is not only unhealthy, but is actually damaging to spiritual life. I do not in any way wish to underestimate the force of the demonic—that indeed is what this book is about—but I do want to emphasise that it is not the whole story. The devil would like us to think it is, because that gives to him far more power than he actually possesses, but before God we need to keep all things in balance. We need constantly to ask God exactly what is happening, because only then will we grow in the way he wants us to—and only then will we be really empowered to serve him, and to stand against whatever the devil may throw at us.

In this respect it is perhaps good to bear in mind the Deuteronomic injunction: 'Know then in your heart that as a man disciplines his son, so the Lord your God disciplines you' (Deuteronomy 8:5).

5. Suffering that comes from evil

This last scenario is included here because it is suffering or pain that is a consequence of sin or wrong choice, but unlike 2 above it is not brought about by God. It properly belongs to the realm of evil, seen as a force working in opposition to God. What happens is that as a result of sin, the devil gains access or right of entry directly into our lives.

His aim is twofold: first, to separate us from God and, second, to focus the worship that rightfully belongs to God upon himself. As he builds up his control, the devil is very good at bestowing an illusion of gifts, all of which to a greater or lesser degree are power based. For example, he may create in individuals the belief that they can, through the performance of certain actions or use of certain objects, influence the health or emotional stability of themselves or others. The longer an individual remains embroiled in this kind of thing, the greater degree of control the devil gets and, at first, the results may seem startling. But the devil is not God. He does not freely give anything, and he cannot create (although he would like to); he can only mangle and destroy.

Once the devil has gained a foothold in our lives, he has every interest in maintaining that hold. He is perfectly happy for us to become adepts in the esoteric arts he gives to us, knowing that in this way he remains the focus of our thoughts and lives. God, however, is not happy for this to continue, and so allows us to suffer the adverse effects of separation. Problems, directly caused by evil, arise when the devil has a foothold in our lives as a result of these wrong choices that have invited him in, and we then turn towards God . . . but without telling the devil to go. We become in every sense at this point a real battleground, with God on the one side fighting for our freedom, and the devil on the other, fighting with no holds barred to draw us away. So let us look briefly at how this situation can arise.

To a certain extent we all have a Russian roulette mentality. We take risks—risks that in our saner moments we know are completely stupid. I am not at all surprised when I hear today that the AIDS epidemic has not affected the sexual behaviour of young people, because within every one of us there is a tendency to think, 'It won't happen to me. It couldn't do! I'm going to get away with it!' So we do things we know to be wrong, even against what God has commanded, and delude ourselves into thinking that it does not really matter. If, however, the unthinkable does happen—we fall ill, for example—no one is surprised, not even ourselves—even though by then we might bitterly regret the actions that have led to this state. These kinds of things are an obvious and logical consequence of sin and it is actually easy, even if painful, to accept when suffering comes as result of something like this. Actually, a situation like this may well bring us back to God, in which case we may well end up thanking him for showing us the error of our ways!

There is, however, a different kind of situation, where there can be intense suffering and pain, and yet the individual concerned has not obviously done the kind of terrible wrong that would merit the hardship they are going through. This, if we are honest, offends our sense of justice, and an almost unbelievable number of people end up blaming God—even while protesting at the same time that they do not believe in him! It is this kind of situation that needs a little unpacking, because what we may well have here is an access point.

It is perfectly possible that what is going on in this situation has actually very little to do with God. It might even offend him, and yet there is very little he can do to intervene—not because he lacks the power, but because we (whether knowingly or unknowingly) are hanging on to whatever it is that has given the devil access . . . which has the result of putting us under the devil's power. This kind of suffering has a demonic source and it is a situation that is far more common than might be supposed. It is the field of battle that Jesus speaks about in the gospels, and it is this kind of hold that the devil has that is the cause of so much suffering and emotional and mental pain in people's lives. We see the effects not just in physical illness, but in things such as broken relationships (especially marriage, and the relationships between parents and children), in anxiety states, in job difficulties, in financial problems, in depression—the list is endless.

What has happened is actually very simple, although some people, for a variety of reasons, find it very hard to accept. When we rebel against God and do wrong, whether we know it or not, we are actually sending out an open invitation to the devil, and he is not slow to take us up on that. Sin gives to the devil an entry into our lives. It enables him to get a hold on us. Unfortunately it is a little bit like throwing a party and having some extremely disruptive gatecrashers turn up. The only way to get rid of them once they have found a way in, is to have some very burly bouncers on site, and until they are actually expelled, they cause endless trouble—in fact the whole party might well disintegrate into chaos. Now the only bouncer with adequate muscle to expel them is Jesus, along with his angelic host. There are, however, several problems. Many people today, even Christians, do not know that the gatecrashers have found a way in, and so have no idea why they are experiencing so much difficulty. Others know that they have arrived, because they can see the effects clearly, but they have absolutely no idea how to deal with them, because they do not actually know God. They might have heard about him, but they have no idea what he is really like, and they have not the faintest idea about obedience. Still others have become so blinded by the effects that they imagine this is the way parties ought to be!

Unrepented sin gives to the devil a hold over us, and this situation has been made ten times worse by the fact that so many of the boundaries between sin and right action have today become hopelessly blurred. Many of us are no longer capable of recognising sin, even when it leaps up and hits us in the face. Just look, for example, at the focus of attention on witches at Hallowe'en, or on the easy acceptance of drugs as a social lubricant at parties, or on the general acceptance that everyone will have had several sexual partners before marriage—if indeed people bother with that institution at all these days. The trouble is that although we might think all these things are harmless, even meaningless, the devil does not. He rightly sees them as giving him a hold over us, and he is in the business of trying to separate us totally from God. Temptation that is demonically inspired seeks to accomplish this, and at the same time to undermine us. And wherever there is unrepented sin present, in whatever form, the devil can and will take advantage.

Moreover, sin does not have to be things such as drug abuse or sexual immorality or dabbling in the occult—all the obvious 'bad' things. Sin includes things such as anger and hatred, or bitterness and resentment. It can even include things like pain and grief, where we are hanging on to these things and letting them sour our life because we just will not or cannot let go. In fact some of these things are not obviously 'bad' at all, but in each case they obscure our perception of God, and give the devil a hold over our lives that has to be broken if we are to be set free.

In the same way, odd as this may sound at first, we can become inheritors of these kinds of holds. Spiritual problems can be passed on from one generation to the next, in much the same way as we now accept an inherited tendency to heart disease or diabetes. Genetics has taught us that the medical conditions we see repeated over and over again within the same family line may actually not be attributable solely to living conditions or diet, but may rather be rooted in some inherited genetic defect: that is, there is an in-built chromosomal weakness or deficiency which, in the absence of external remedial intervention, predisposes the individual to the development of the particular disease concerned. In the same way, it seems, spiritual holds can be passed on from one generation to the next and predispose the individual to fall prey to the same kind of sin and endure the same pattern of suffering. Unrepented sin opens up an access point for the devil through which he can wreak havoc, not just upon an individual, but down a whole family line—he thinks he owns that line! It is a part of the outworking of the proverb found repeated twice in the Old Testament: 'The fathers eat sour grapes, and the children's teeth are set on edge' (Ezekiel 18:2; Jeremiah 31:29).

This proverb appears to have achieved widespread popularity within Israel at around the time of the destruction of Jerusalem in 587 BC. The people apparently felt that their doom was imminent, and that it was punishment—not for anything they had done, but for the accumulated sins of their forefathers. Then, when their worst fears were realised and they had suffered the most appalling military defeat at the hands of the Babylonians, the Lord spoke to them. I am going to break this, he said, because every living soul belongs to me. You are not going to suffer for the sins others have committed, but only for your own (see Ezekiel 18:3–24).

The point is, it took God's intervention to break the cycle of cause and effect set up here. The people's sin arose because of their disobedience to God's commands, but the punishment once initiated appears to have had its own momentum, and God said that this was not right; what he required was the faithfulness of each individual, and it was by that that he would judge them. So on the one hand we have God's withdrawal of protection where the people have been disobedient, but on the other we have a punishment of such extreme savagery that it goes far beyond what the Lord will countenance as just. In the same way for us, where there is sin, God responds in the way that is appropriate to correct and actually help us, but this sin at the same time gives the devil an opportunity to leap in and cause havoc. His field of influence is not simply limited to the individual concerned, but through that individual he can reach down to their children, and their children's children. It is because we are created by God as spiritual beings, and he has set within us a spiritual continuity with our children and those we love. It is part of the way God has made not just us, but the whole of creation.

From the very first, men and women were intended by God to live in community and fellowship with one another. We were never intended to live in isolation—which is precisely why, having created Adam, God then created Eve . . . not just as some kind of inferior bricky's mate, but because without Eve, Adam was incomplete. Eve was a part of Adam. He could not live without her, and there is certainly no way she could ever have existed without him, as she was created from him. They were mutually interrelated and dependent and, whether we like it or not, spiritually it's exactly the same for all of us today. We are all interrelated, and that is why our unrepented sin can have such a powerful effect on our children, and why we in turn can be so powerfully affected by the unrepented sins of others in our families. That spiritual interrelatedness is one of the greatest gifts of God and a means by which his blessings are given, but it is also one which the devil is very quick to exploit for his own ends.

Not so long ago a lady, whom I shall call Gwen, came to see me. She was very worried because her daughter was anorexic and sinking further and further into depression. 'I find it so upsetting,' she said, 'because she's so very like me. It's like looking at myself, and I *blame* myself for all of this, because somehow I've got the most awful feeling that I've caused it all.' At which point she began to cry. It emerged that in her childhood and early teens she had been badly abused. Her mother had known, and hated her for it, and eventually her father had been sent to prison. But what also emerged was that this pattern of incest went back through several generations—as far back in fact as the family records went. Members from each generation had also suffered from acute depression and there had been at least one suicide directly resulting from the family situation. In some form the general pattern had affected each and every member of that family, both males and females alike. Her own marriage, hardly surprisingly, was deeply unhappy, and now she was terrified, because she saw the same pattern becoming set in her own children (she had a son as well as a daughter).

The point is that the sins apparently first committed by her ancestors some three or four generations before had, from that time, given the devil a stranglehold on her whole family, and that hold had to be broken. They had to be set free from all of that, and allowed in God to stand as individuals. Where this kind of generational hold has been established, it is only God who can break it. Counselling alone, although it may well be needed to help the individual adjust once set free, will achieve nothing; the hold has to be smashed.

As I was thinking and praying about this whole area, and exactly how the devil gains access into our lives, in what seemed almost like confirmation I had an unexpected phone call from a friend, Chris. Chris had absolutely no idea what I was writing about, although she knew about the book, but she said that she had just been having her quiet time with God when she had felt him telling her to phone me. She said that as she had been sitting musing, she had begun to think about the devil—in particular how he works, and how very attractive his lures can sometimes be. She had recently been watching a popular fictional series on television about the devil and his attempts to capture the souls of three girls, but that morning as she sat praying it had suddenly struck her, completely out of the blue, how very attractive the devil can appear, and how extremely reasonable his temptations to sin can be. And of course that is absolutely right—sin does not always appear to be obviously wrong. It can seem eminently attractive, even sensible.

However, two further things had struck Chris, and it was because of these that she had felt impelled to call. The first was that in this televised story the devil drove a car, into which he kept trying to lure one particular girl. It was only when she accepted his invitation and got into the car that he actually held any power over her. This is exactly how sin operates. The devil can tempt us but, as emphasised above, he holds absolutely no power until we succumb. When we do succumb, however, his power is very great, and this was Chris' second point. As soon as this girl got into the car, the devil held power not only over her, but also over the two friends whom she loved and was closest to. When she succumbed, he could *and did* intervene in their lives too. At times he gave apparent gifts as a part of his lure, and at other times, when the girl he was trying to ensnare resisted, he upended all of their lives with disaster.

Now this was, as I have said, a televised novel and the analogy should not be stretched too far, but the underlying principle is absolutely right. Sin in the first instance does not have to appear bad. While we resist, the devil holds no power over us—although he can still attack us from outside. It is only when we succumb that we sin and the devil gains power over us. While that sin remains, it is an access point for the devil, not only into our own lives, but into the lives of our children and grandchildren and beyond.

To make a slightly different but not entirely unconnected point here, it is worth commenting that unrepented sin would appear sometimes to open up an avenue for demonic attack upon those we love, or are otherwise close to, but to whom we are genetically unrelated. This, I believe, is especially true between husbands and wives, but it operates also on a wider level. A good example of this is seen in the apocryphal story, Tobit. There the young girl, Sarah, is oppressed by the demon Asmodeus. The demon does not hurt her, but each time she is given in marriage, out of jealousy, he kills the spouse on the wedding night. The point would appear to be that he gains the power to destroy the husbands by the act of marriage. The cycle is ended only when Tobias (her eighth husband) defeats the demon with the help of the angel Raphael, and she is set free.

Now Tobit, of course, does not have the same status as the canonical books and we should not make the mistake of treating it as Scripture, but we have already seen how the sin of Achan in Joshua 6 brought down God's judgement upon the whole Jewish nation, even though they were unaware of the offence. I believe that what we are seeing in this kind of situation is the reverse side of the same coin. God withdraws his protection in order to expose the sin, and the devil leaps in. He does not have carte blanche to oppress people, of course, but most certainly the sin makes available to him an avenue through which he can wreak havoc. It should be stressed that at no point is he in control of the situation—although it can feel like it at the time! Actually, he is simply exploiting areas of potential weakness that already exist.

To give two examples of this: a while ago I was involved in ministry to a young woman who was severely spiritually oppressed. Her husband was a clergyman. Over the course of about five years his ministry had been totally smashed by a series of bizarre and seemingly unconnected events. It became apparent, however, that at least some of those events were rooted in the spiritual oppression that had been affecting his wife. On another occasion, I was approached by a young woman asking for prayer after a meeting I had been addressing. She told me that the rector's wife at the church she attended, was apparently involved in a lesbian relationship with another member of the fellowship. This had understandably produced a lot of tension, but more recently things had started to go badly wrong with the church as a whole. In particular three marriages had disintegrated within the last couple of months and a spiritual deadness seemed to have settled on the worship. Hardly surprising, perhaps, when you think about it, but what most concerned this lady (apart from her deep feelings of distress at the whole situation) was that she felt the Lord had said to her that what was happening was a direct consequence of the sin attaching to the leadership. Was this fanciful? I believe not. The devil is very quick to exploit situations to which he has been given access, and he will most certainly try to destroy the things that bring us closer to God—and God will allow this in order to purify and recall us to himself.

Whether we like it or not, then, this life is a battleground. There is no neutral area where we are 'safe'. We have to decide which side we are on, and while we remain uncommitted, the devil gives no quarter. Much, even most, of the pain, suffering and difficulty we encounter in life *does* originate with the devil.

Now, having set the field, we need to examine exactly who and what this 'person' is.

4
Who Is the Devil?

The ancient Israelites had a problem with evil. It was undeniably there, but God, as he had revealed himself to them, was the one and only Creator God—so far above all other gods as to make their petty pretensions entirely devoid of either meaning or power. It is difficult today to grasp how very revolutionary such a belief system would have been to the ancient world, but the idea of there being only one God would have been radical in the extreme. True, we see movements towards this kind of belief in other religious systems—the Egyptians, for example, under Amenophis IV (Akhenaten) were moving towards the idea of there being one supreme deity—but as consistently expressed by the Jews, such a belief was entirely without precedent.

They held to it, of course, because that was the way 'Yahweh', the God who will be what he will be, had revealed himself to them. Their belief was not just the product of a group of wise men sitting down and thinking about it, but came from their experience of Yahweh's dealings with them. And that in itself says something of fundamental importance to our belief today, because any belief only becomes real faith when it is grounded in personal experience. Once people have had that kind of experience, then even though in this life it will be limited, they have to keep faith with the revelation God has given to them, even though this may well be extremely hard—as the Jews found to their cost when coming up against the thoughts and beliefs of the peoples round about.

Yahweh, supremely in the Exodus, had revealed himself to them not only as their deliverer, but as the one and only true God—supreme even over all the gods of other nations. Their problem, then, was very simple. If Yahweh was the one and only true God, wholly good and supreme over all other powers, how was it that there was so much evil in the world? It was easy for the other religious systems, because they had no problem in seeing evil either as an essential part of reality, along with all that was good, so that the two lived in balance, together making one harmonious whole, or in attributing disaster to the malign workings of some ill-intentioned or blood-thirsty god, who was merely one from among a far larger pantheon.

Certainly, in relation to the latter view, the gods of other belief systems were capricious in the extreme. They were very similar in their emotions to human beings and so warred among themselves and suffered relational disputes, and generally acted in what frequently seems a most immoral manner. It was the work of pagan priests to try to keep at bay the forces of chaos stirred up by these beings, and that inhered naturally in the cosmic sphere, threatening at any moment to overthrow the stability of both nature and the social order. To this end they therefore attempted, through the performance of rite, to gain some kind of handle on these unpredictable deities, and facilitate the unobstructed flow of divine power into the material world, of which the seasons, the political order and the social fabric were all a part. If the priests failed in their rituals, then the whole structure underpinning this flow was weakened, and it was believed that all kinds of disasters would follow.

In Canaanite myth, for example, second only to the great god El, it was believed that the ruling deity, Baal (also known as the storm god Hadad), owned the land and controlled its fertility. His consort was the female deity Ashtart (or Astarte). Each year, in the cycle of the seasons, the people saw mirrored their sacred marriage. In this cycle of dependency, it was believed that new life came to nature as a result of sexual union between these two. On their fecundity depended the fruitfulness of the land. In their ritual, then, the Canaanites sought, by their re-enactment of the turbulent relationship between Baal and Ashtart, to facilitate the coming together of the divine pair in fertilising union. Strange as it may seem today, it was believed that by imitating the actions of these two gods within the cult, power would be released within the divine sphere to bring about the desired union.

The Ras Shamra texts found at Ugarit (an ancient Canaanite city) and dating from about 1400 BC give the most amazing picture of early Canaanite religion, but it is worth noting that although the names are different, the same myths are found also in both Babylon (Tammuz and Ishtar) and Egypt (Osiris and Isis). According to these texts, the high god who ruled all the others in a kind of loose if rather turbulent democracy was El, while his consort was named Asherah. Next in rank to him was Baal, the storm god. His consort, Ashtart or Anath, was also his sister, and she was a war goddess, noted both for her unbridled sexual passions and her extreme brutality. According to myth, Baal came to pre-eminence following his defeat of the water dragon (the almost universal symbol in the ancient world for chaos—which, as we shall see, also has a bearing on Jewish thought). For a time all went well and then Mot, the god of summer drought, in turn grew jealous, attacked and killed Baal—now recognised as the lord of the earth—and carried him down to the underworld. Ashtart was bereft at this and set out to search for Baal. When she at last found him, captive in the underworld, she attacked Mot and after a terrible battle defeated him, thus allowing for Baal's resurrection and his reassumption of power.

There was no way that the Jews could subscribe to these kinds of ideas and still remain true to their faith—both in God and in the essential nature not only of mankind but of the whole of creation. The problem of evil was there at the dawn of creation, true, but for them it was not inherent in matter. So we see in the Bible a rather subtle picture. On the one hand the presence of evil is an enigma, but at the same time it is given a definite historical beginning—and that beginning and activity is essentially scandalous. However you look at it, there is no way it should be there.

The writer of Genesis is categorical in insisting that God alone created the heavens and the earth, calling forth matter out of chaos, and that it was and is wholly good: 'God saw all that he had made, and it was very good' (Genesis 1:31). It is against this backdrop then that the serpent appeared and began his apparently causeless seduction of Eve.

In the creation account the serpent is at no point equated with the devil. Genesis 3:1 simply says, '. . . the serpent was more crafty than any of the wild animals the Lord God had made.' The serpent is therefore presented as entirely the handiwork of God, and at no point is there any suggestion of evil, as some extraneous force equal to God, invading from outside. To all appearances, Eve is tempted by a creature entirely her subordinate. The decision to rebel is her own, and the evil, as manifested, is her rejection of the order that God has laid down for the right functioning of his world.

There are, however, hints from the text that there is something rather deeper going on here. To begin with, the designation of the serpent as the instrument of temptation would have evoked an immediate response in the minds of the first listeners or readers, because throughout the ancient Near East, the figure of the snake was inextricably bound with pagan fertility cults. It was the symbol for all things associated with the occult, divination and magic, representing the powerful divinities of the ground. As a symbol it would have encapsulated the essence of pagan rite and belief, powerfully evoking the darker practices explicitly forbidden by Yahweh to the Jews. But even more convincing that there is something more at stake here is the curse God specifically pronounces against the snake: 'Cursed are you above all the livestock and all the wild animals! You will crawl on your belly and you will eat dust all the days of your life. And I will put enmity between you and the woman, and between your offspring and hers; he will crush your head, and you will strike his heel' (Genesis 3:14–15).

No creature in the normal course of events would have had the kind of lifespan hinted at here, but the judgement God pronounces is very specifically aimed at the individual person of the snake. In the curse he utters, God first promises that men and women will be protected from falling entirely under the domination of the snake, by the simple device of placing enmity between the offspring of both. Second, he makes a categorical assertion of final, *personal* defeat. Now there is no suggestion here of possession, but without a doubt from the framing of the words, the text hints at another figure behind that of the snake. The snake is a being bearing responsibility (God would not otherwise have specifically pronounced judgement upon it) in which connection it is also interesting to note that it is the snake he curses first before Eve and then Adam, thus establishing priority of blame as attaching first and foremost to the tempter, whose ruse in trying to draw Adam and Eve to his side in rebellion against God is thus exposed.

For their part, Adam and Eve have without doubt succumbed to the initial temptation and in that way have fundamentally ruptured the conditions under which they live and—even more importantly—their standing before God. But the Lord God does not abandon them. He demonstrates his ultimate and irrevocable control over the serpent and the being behind it, by in that very moment promising final redemption, albeit only after the passage of many generations. God's punishment of the snake in this way suggests not any evil or weakness inherent in reality, but a particular agent working to undermine and despoil. It suggests in fact the workings of the adversary, only finally and totally unmasked in the coming of Jesus—the one who does crush the enemy's head in fulfilment of God's prophecy, albeit at the cost of his own life. The curse pronounced here explicitly against the serpent therefore becomes in turn a symbol and prophecy for the deeper punishment pronounced by God upon the evil one—the real prime mover in this drama.

From that point, the identification of the serpent with the adversary unfolds only gradually in Scripture (eg Isaiah 27:1). Fairly consistently, however, evil rapidly becomes identified with Leviathan—the great dragon, the chaos monster, all of them powerful variations on the snake—again, each one a symbol of the demonic and horrific spirit at the heart of paganism. Yet it is only in Revelation that we have the final and explicit identification made: 'The great dragon was hurled down—that ancient serpent called the devil, or Satan, who leads the whole world astray. He was hurled to the earth, and his angels with him' (Revelation 12:9. cf. 20:2).

It is perhaps fitting and a part of God's protection of mankind that the full conflict with the adversary is only finally and fully unmasked with the coming of his Son, while it is only given full definition in the great prophetic work that stands at the end of Scripture. Even given this, however, it should not be thought that the Old Testament does not have very important things to say about the nature and workings of the devil, and of his standing before God.

So Satan is powerful and stands in opposition to God. He attempts to pervert and destroy the things of God and, especially, to rupture our relationship with our Maker and Father; his aim in fact is to hijack the worship and love we should in the normal course of events give to God, and focus it upon himself. But his power games are ultimately power-less before the might of God. Only God has real power, because only God can create and establish order. The satan is himself a created being and as such, no matter how much he dislikes that fact, he is ultimately under God's authority.

Consider the now all-too-familiar scenario of a boardroom battle. One of the most senior executives has secretly attempted to launch a takeover bid. He has bought up shares, and been very busy getting different members of both the board and the workforce on his side, telling them that the Chairman's day is over and it's his turn now. When the Chairman finally comes into the room, however, the executive collapses, simply because it was not true—he never did have the power. Other members of the board by themselves did not have the power to deal with this upstart. They could resist him, but it took the Chairman himself, and the one to whom he specifically delegated authority, to deal with him.

What we see in Eden is the devil's attempt at a takeover bid—very subtle and without any obvious aggression, but no less real for all that. And he damages the company. The Chairman, however, is still very much in control and this recalcitrant board member still has to obey him, even though at the same time he works unsparingly to cause trouble. Yet at every moment God knows exactly what his enemy is up to. God uses him at times, but he also promises his children—the members of his company who remain loyal—that he will protect them and give them power to resist . . . and not only to resist, but to overcome and stand safe whenever the devil sees fit to launch one of his ploys. But the final defeat only comes when God himself, in Jesus, moves to crush the upstart.

Seen in this light, various references in Scripture take on the most tremendous power. Look, for example, at the promise of Psalm 91:13, 'You will tread upon the lion and the cobra; you will trample the great lion and the serpent.' What we have here is nothing less than

God's absolute promise, yet again, of triumph over the adversary.

There are, then, several points that arise from any analysis of the Fall narrative and Eden. First, the moral evil that is undeniably present in the world arises from rebellion among God's creatures. Second, the force of evil external to men and women has its origins in an order of creation separate from ourselves, but without a doubt still under the lordship of God, and dependent on him for its being. Third, the underlying impulse of that external force is aimed at undermining and despoiling God's handiwork, and its chief weapons are the assertion of autonomy and doubt of God's love. Seen in another light, the aim of the enemy, as already mentioned, is to divert worship from God to himself. Fourth, and most importantly, the activities of the adversary are covert. His attack upon Eve takes the form of a temptation that is subtle in the extreme. He implants a suggestion in her mind that has its own momentum and pressure, but at no point does he appear obviously evil or in direct opposition to God.

One of the greatest problems in dealing with evil is that it is often very difficult to pin down. To our confusion, it can frequently appear eminently reasonable—even moved by proper concern—but it sows seeds of doubt that disable and ultimately destroy, shattering unity. Sometimes, of course, it is entirely right and God-given to question what is going on, or the rightness of a projected plan; but not always. One of the ways of discerning whether doubts, criticisms or questionings are or are not of God is to ask yourself whether they are being made openly—and whether they are actually being addressed to the person against whom they are directed. *Anything* that works by stealth and is not open is not of God and should be avoided. It will cause harm. What is actually tremendous evil often works through subtle plottings and suggestion, but when confronted it evaporates or hides behind subterfuge and smiles. We should make no mistake: evil is real, it is directed, and it is very hard to deal with, precisely because it so often pretends to be what it is not. But God promises us that if we remain obedient to him, he will give us discernment to recognise the enemy—and that promise is made in Genesis when the enemy first appears. In the first instance, ours is the fault if we succumb.

Having said that, however, spiritually things are not always quite that easy, simply because the devil can and frequently does get a hold over our emotions and our minds, which can lead to ingrained patterns of behaviour from which it is very difficult to break free. Precisely what this means and how that breaking free is accomplished, we shall address later (see Chapters 12 and 13). For the moment we are focusing solely on the person and reality of the devil, for if evil arises from rebellion among God's creatures, we need to know a little more about the creature who first rebelled.

Before we look in more detail at what the Old Testament has to tell us about this personage, it is helpful to look first at some of the early Hebrew traditions, because although frequently not directly incorporated into Scripture, they had a real effect on both the thought and belief of the early writers and religious leaders. The stories indeed would have been known to all, and although not given the status of holy Scripture, they were given high standing in Jewish belief, frequently underlying many of what appear to be the more abstruse passages in Scripture. To know these traditions is not only to have a clearer idea of exactly how the first believers viewed the devil, but also to understand more clearly where some of our own ideas and beliefs come from.

Lucifer

In rabbinic myth there are a variety of traditions identifying Satan, though all agree that he is a fallen angel (for a more detailed discussion of angels see Chapter 9). One tradition specifically refers to him as God's chief archangel, a cherub named Lucifer, son of the Dawn (Helel ben Shahar). As the story runs, on the third day of creation, while walking in Eden and clothed in brilliant jewels, Lucifer suddenly fell prey to overweening pride. He decided he was so glorious that he was just as worthy of worship as God (one variation of this particular tradition says that God had actually appointed Lucifer to oversee and rule the earth). This cherub grew inordinately jealous of God and without more ado determined to ascend above the clouds and stars and enthrone himself on Saphon, the Mount of Assembly, thus setting himself up as God's equal. There and then God cast Lucifer down, first from Eden to earth, and from there to Sheol—the bottomless pit. Lucifer, the tradition runs, shone like lightning as he fell, but was reduced in the process to ashes, his beauty utterly spoiled.

The interesting thing about this particular tradition is that it surfaces obscurely in both Isaiah and Ezekiel, but in both the references are unmistakable. In the prophecy against Babylon in Isaiah 14:12–15, for example, the fall of the King of Babylon is specifically likened to that of Helel ben Shahar:

> How you have fallen from heaven,
>   O morning star, son of the dawn!
> You have been cast down to the earth,
>   you who once laid low the nations!
> You said in your heart,
>   'I will ascend to heaven;
> I will raise my throne
>   above the stars of God;
> I will sit enthroned on the mount of assembly,
>   on the utmost heights of the sacred mountain.
> I will ascend above the tops of the clouds;
>   I will make myself like the Most High.'
> But you are brought down to the grave,
>   to the depths of the pit.

Of particular note is the fact that the King of Babylon is at this point totally identified with Lucifer, carrying the suggestion that behind this entirely worldly figure stands an even greater spiritual force. In his pride and arrogance the King of Babylon has become not just an instrument in Lucifer's hands, but the tangible outworking of his directing power, resulting from total identification of will. This king is someone who, through his pride, has totally surrendered himself to demonic control, and who therefore himself now stands in total opposition to God.

A similar identification is found in Ezekiel 28:11–19, though here relating to the King of Tyre. The first ten verses of the chapter particularly relate to the earthly figure of the king, but thereafter the chapter continues;

> You were the model of perfection,
>   full of wisdom and perfect in beauty.
> You were in Eden,
>   the garden of God;
> every precious stone adorned you . . .

You were anointed as a guardian cherub,
   for so I ordained you.
You were on the holy mount of God;
   you walked among the fiery stones.
You were blameless in your ways
   from the day you were created
   till wickedness was found in you.
Through your widespread trade
   you were filled with violence,
   and you sinned.
So I drove you in disgrace from the mount of God . . .
I threw you to the earth.

Again, there is a complete identification of will here between the earthly ruler of Tyre (who has taken over the spiritual aspirations of his master) and the rebellious cherub prince, once perfect, who in his pride defied God—and against both the same judgement is pronounced. The identification is explicit—behind the arrogant King of Tyre stands Satan himself.

This in itself tells us something about power. When properly exercised, it is not bad, but all power on this earth is exercised only under authority. The picture is clearly painted in Scripture. The first authority for the exercise of power comes from God's command to Adam: 'God blessed them and said to them, "Be fruitful and increase in number; fill the earth and subdue it. Rule over the fish of the sea and the birds of the air and over every living creature that moves on the ground"' (Genesis 1:28).

Evil takes root when men and women are tempted to try and arrogate that power to themselves, leaving God out of the picture. But men and women simply do not have the standing to take that kind of power for themselves. More than that, they can attempt it only at the instigation of some other manipulating force. To flout God's authority is to become subject to the authority of another. At no point do men and women stand alone in some kind of moral and spiritual vacuum. We simply do not have a choice about this. We are either under the authority of God (and protected) or under the influence and sway of the devil. That influence does not immediately become total once we have succumbed, because God's love still reaches out to us, but it means that from that point there is a real spiritual conflict going on. The kings of Babylon and Tyre, referred to in these two passages, have so completely given themselves over to the sway of Satan that they have fallen completely under his power . . . to the extent that they have now become extensions of him.

Over the past couple of years much has been made of the idea of cities, places and institutions having their own ruling demon standing behind the secular powers. We shall explore this idea, and in particular its theological backing, in greater detail in Chapter 10. For the present the point to be made is that the kings of Babylon and Tyre had opened themselves up to this kind of hold by their total rejection of even nominal obedience to God. The absolute identification of will made here between themselves and Satan is therefore unusual in its totality. Nevertheless, the picture that we have from Scripture is that the guiding force behind any power that is not in obedience to God, although it does not necessarily imply control, is always that which is in rebellion—there is no area of neutrality—and the prince of rebellion is Satan.

We find a further possible reference to this same tradition on the lips of Jesus in Luke 10:18: 'I saw Satan fall like lightning from heaven.' The exact meaning of this verse is obscure. Many Bible commentators suggest that it is perhaps a prophetic vision on Jesus' part of Satan's final defeat, referring to the war in heaven. Almost certainly, however, Jesus would have had in mind the passages cited above from Isaiah and Ezekiel, in which case his words tell us things of profound importance relating both to Satan and to himself. Seen in the light of the tradition, his words in fact take on the meaning: 'I was there in heaven when Satan first rebelled. I saw the beginnings of the battle. I saw Satan, for his presumption, thrown from his eternal home to earth. The battle still rages, but now I have come, and I give to you my eternal authority (that originates in those same heavenly places) to overcome all the enemy's power.'

Jesus would most certainly have known both the Scriptures and the tradition. So too would his disciples. If then this is the tradition to which he was referring, it shows Jesus identifying Satan with Lucifer. If this is right, it tells us something very important about Jesus' own view of the origins and nature of evil.

Of course there are some today who would not be impressed by this point, arguing that Jesus' worldview was clearly shaped by the essentially superstitious character of the age in which he lived. We run into problems, however, if we decide to be selective in distinguishing between those things in the Bible (and more particularly on the lips of Jesus) which we consider to be intellectually 'sound' and those we feel to be suspect on the grounds that they do not correspond to our own worldview. On this line of approach any teaching in the Bible becomes open to question. Moreover, such an attitude is actually to deny God the foresight and understanding both to compensate for and work through this. It is in fact to divest God of his divinity, questioning his capacity for accurate self-revelation. Whether we like it or not, Jesus did take the existence and activity of Satan very seriously indeed, and we should therefore resist the temptation to jettison so completely what he has to say.

Non-biblical stories

A second rabbinic tradition that deserves attention is that relating to another archangel, Samael. According to this tradition Samael was provoked to rebellion on account of his jealousy for Adam. On the sixth day, the story runs, God created Adam and was so pleased with his handiwork that he ordered the host of heaven to bow down and worship him. Samael took exception to this and refused, saying that Adam ought rather to worship him. The Archangel Michael then warned him to beware God's anger, eliciting a response from Samael along the lines of, 'Let him try!' This so incensed Michael that he threw his fellow down to earth, where Samael—now openly in rebellion—continued to scheme against God. In some parts of Hebrew myth, the serpent in Eden is therefore identified with Samael in disguise.

Yet another tradition, and one far closer to the dualistic myths of the Hebrew nation's ancient Middle Eastern neighbours, identifies Satan with the Prince of Darkness, seen here as a positive entity and not as the mere absence of light. In this tradition, the Prince of Darkness opposed God when the latter determined to create his world in light. In response God confined him, along with his angels, to a dark dungeon. The myth, however, does not end here. In the last days the Prince will break free, rising to challenge God as his equal on the grounds that although God has created heaven and light, he has 'created' darkness and the pit. A struggle for supremacy is foretold, but one in which God will triumph.

This is clearly a totally different strand of thought, but it is interesting for what it has to say about hell. Almost without thinking we see Satan today as the ruler of hell, but Scripture actually presents a very different picture. We shall examine the exact relationship between Satan and the pit in Chapter 8, but it is a point obviously of tremendous importance—not only for spiritual warfare, but also in shaping our own view of judgement and the resurrection.

These then are the main traditions behind the figure of Lucifer or Satan that we find in the Bible (Hebrew myth contains many more stories relating to the nature and function of angels, both as serving God and as having given allegiance to the devil). The clear point to be made, however, is that whatever Satan's precise origins, he is always conceived of in Hebrew tradition and belief as a being created by God. He does not in himself have any powers of creativity, although he is consumed with jealousy when he contemplates the handiwork of God and would clearly like to have this power. His desire is to be equal with God and a focus of the worship that properly belongs to the Maker. To this end the devil therefore tries to undermine what God has made, inciting others of God's creatures to reject his authority and live in disobedience. He is eternal, but he is neither omnipresent nor omniscient, although as a guardian cherub he undeniably has power. Though he abuses that power, in the last analysis he remains under the authority of God.

Having seen what there is to be learned from myth, we need now to turn to the broader canvas of the Old Testament to see how this is worked out in the centuries leading up to the coming of Christ.

The Old Testament view of Satan

In the Old Testament, the name 'the satan' simply means 'the adversary or accuser'. He is a part of the heavenly council and, where he appears, his function is to test the faithful by accusing them before God, or by seeing if they can be led astray through temptation. There is constant rebellion on the part of the Israelites against Yahweh (eg, in Judges we find the often-repeated phrase: 'The Israelites once again did evil in the eyes of the Lord'—see Judges 4:1; 6:1; 10:6, etc), but there is never at any point a sense of focused evil working in deliberate opposition to God. There is of course a strong awareness of pagan gods—and in common perception these were clearly seen as wielding a certain amount of power (see for example the power struggle between Elijah and the prophets of Baal in 1 Kings 18), but there is never any link made between these and some cosmological force of evil standing in opposition to God.

The role of the satan is perhaps most clearly seen in Job, where he is specifically referred to in the Hebrew as one of the sons of God—a term generally used in the Old Testament for angels (see Job 1:6). In this book there is a certain opposition in the satan's manner, not just towards Job, but also towards God, yet he still cannot operate beyond the limits of God's express permission. So we find a certain ambiguity. He is hostile and he is powerful, but at the same time he is God's servant and cannot operate beyond the limits of God's will. Although he causes harm, he is not specifically identified with evil.

In Job, God permits the satan's testing of his faithful servant only in order to vindicate Job's righteousness, and the fact that God can have a free loving relationship with man without having to buy it. It is important to note that at no point does God will Job harm. At no point does he feel anger towards Job. On the contrary, he is extremely pleased with him and permits the testing only because the satan derides Job's apparent faithfulness, attributing it not to love of God, but rather to self-interest. The satan's attack is therefore very much the outcome of hostility, and although God permits it, his activities are at all times kept very firmly within bounds.

However, in the Old Testament, although clearly opposed to men and women, the satan's activities are not always hostile to God. A rather different perspective is, for example, given in 1 Chronicles 21:1. In this passage it is Satan (and this is the only passage in the Old Testament where Satan is used as a proper name) who incites David to take a census of Israel in complete disregard to God's will. But there is no suggestion here of either antagonism or opposition to God, and interestingly, in the parallel passage in 2 Samuel 24:1, it is God himself who incites David to disobedience—because he is angry with Israel.

The difference of presentation between these two stories has to do with a developing consciousness of evil. Chronicles was written in post-exilic times when, as result of Babylonian influence, there was a much sharper consciousness of evil as a distinct and separate force. This is not to suggest that there was any radical discontinuity of perception, nor that the Jews had taken over Babylonian cosmology. Rather, what we are seeing is a more defined expression of the same basic view, but with the personality behind the satan now in far sharper focus as a distinct entity.

Thus, to the ancient Israelites, God was seen as controlling both good and evil. The satan was his servant, even while at times appearing to be his foe. Nothing could happen without God's express command, as echoed in Amos 3:6, 'When disaster comes to a city, has not the Lord caused it?'

The satan appears on only one other occasion in the Old Testament, and that is in the book of Zechariah, where he stands at the right hand of Joshua the high priest, to 'accuse him' (Zechariah 3:1; cf. Psalm 109:6). The setting may be the heavenly council, as at the beginning of Job, with Yahweh surrounded by his angelic host. Satan, the adversary of both Israel and all humankind would appear to hold rightful place in this company. In this passage, however, a real conflict has become apparent within that council—a struggle between good and evil on a cosmic scale, with the future of Israel held in the balance. Joshua, the high priest, here seen as representing Israel and so stained with guilt, stands within the clutches of Satan because of that guilt and is saved only by the Lord himself intervening to rebuke his accuser. At the Lord's command Joshua is stripped of his filthy clothes, purified of all sin and dressed in clean clothes. The stripping of his clothes symbolically removes from him the contagion of evil; now Satan can no longer lay any kind of claim to him. So here we have a definite progression in perception. Satan has become an adversary, in every sense hostile to mankind. He remains obedient to God, in so far as his actions are curtailed by God, but in his hostility towards man there is evidence of a struggle for possession, with Satan laying before the Lord what he regards as his legitimate claim. His claim is cancelled only with the stripping away of Joshua's sin.

So then, although the Old Testament does not tell us very much about Satan, what it does have to say is clearly of relevance to our understanding of the devil today. The picture we have is of a spiritual being with immense power, but he is created—he is one of God's heavenly host—and the power he wields is at every point subject to the will of God. Yet in the Old Testament the satan is at no point specifically identified with either Lucifer or Samael. Rather, the satan appears to be simply an angelic office—an official accuser or prosecutor. Whether the term refers simply to one or several angels is not clear. What is clear is that this angel accuser is generally hostile—something that becomes progressively apparent. However, although he can undeniably cause havoc, he can lay claim only where there is sin. The Lord alone can cancel that claim, and he does so by the removal of sin, and by cleansing the individual concerned.

The devil in the New Testament is much more frightening, but the insights gleaned from the Old Testament remain true. Satan's power is undeniably great, but limited, and he does not possess the power of creation. He can only attempt to despoil and pervert, and he can get a hold only through sin. Where there is unrepented sin, he stakes what he asserts is a legitimate claim, and it is there that we see the battle fought for the souls of men and women. At other times he attempts to harry the faithful. His motives are hostile and he hopes, by the temptation to sin, to gain a hold over us and spoil the purposes of God. God at times permits this testing, but like Lazarus called forth into new life, where he allows it, it is ultimately only for our good . . . though that is not to say that, like Job, we shall not experience pain.

Evil spirits

In the Old Testament the work of the satan—the adversary—is to accuse and harry. Quite apart from this, however, the Lord would appear to have a number of other evil spirits at his command. The activities of these spirits would appear to be both distinct and separate. For example, after Saul has been anointed by Samuel as future king over Israel, the Spirit of God comes upon him in power at Gibeah, both to affirm and enable him to fulfil the role he is now called to (1 Samuel 10:9–11). As king, however, Saul displeases God because he sets out to establish Israel as a secular power, and in the process disobeys the Lord's express commands at almost every turn. In fairness to Saul, he is not aware of the evil he is doing—he simply does not realise what obedience to the Lord really means. He appears, in fact, to imagine that a kind of loose obedience will be enough and that because he is king he can do anything—even to the extent of taking over Samuel's role and offering sacrifice. What he fails to appreciate is that, in taking upon himself this role of absolute monarch, he is usurping the position that rightfully belongs to God, and it is this that provokes God's wrath. The result is that the Lord rejects Saul as king (1 Samuel

15:10–23), sending Samuel to anoint David instead. It is at this point we read that the Spirit of the Lord leaves Saul, and in its place the Lord sends an evil spirit to torment him (1 Samuel 16:14f.).

This spirit would appear to induce in Saul a kind of paranoid depression that is soothed only by music. So we read that whenever it comes upon Saul, it is driven out only when David plays his harp (1 Samuel 16:23–24). The Lord, however, gives Saul up to the domination of this spirit so that he descends deeper and deeper into madness, becoming in the process insanely jealous of David. Saul's lot is ultimately tragic. Although not directly attributed to the activity of this spirit, we know that in the end he takes his own life (1 Samuel 31:1–6) and it is clear throughout that this fate has only come upon him because of his disobedience to the Lord.

Saul's descent into madness is then the Lord's judgement for sin. It is brought about by an evil spirit under the direct command of the Lord. This is saying something very important to us today. Sin provokes God's judgement and, unfashionable though it may seem, there is no getting away from that. God takes sin very seriously—if he did not, he would not have sent his own Son to bear the penalty on the cross. Jesus takes sin seriously, and we are simply deluding ourselves if we say certain things do not matter. Disobedience and sin produce suffering—not always immediately, but inevitably. This does not mean that we have to live in a state of abject terror, imagining that our every act is being weighed in some celestial scale of judgement that will bring down divine retribution at any moment—but where suffering is the result of sin (and it needs the Lord's discernment to be able to see this), it can be healed and removed only by repentance.

Again an evil spirit is seen in 1 Kings 22:1–28 (and the parallel passage in 2 Chronicles 18:1–27). In judgement upon Ahab, the Lord allows a lying spirit to enter the mouths of the 400 prophets the king consults in order to learn whether or not he will have victory in the war against Ramoth Gilead. Micaiah, apparently the only genuine prophet of the Lord (the implication would appear to be that the other prophets were of Baal), says to Ahab, 'The Lord has put a lying spirit in the mouths of all these prophets of yours. The Lord has decreed disaster for you' (1 Kings 22:23).

There is a paradox here, but for us the important point to note is that not all apparent evil is directly caused by the devil. Indeed, in some situations it would appear to be in the devil's interest to try and prevent suffering, because it is that which alerts us to the fact that we are out of step with God, and that something is deeply wrong. There is something important here, and extremely relevant to our lives today.

I have heard it said that we can judge things by their effects. Now at one level this is entirely accurate and has sound scriptural backing (see Matthew 7:16). But at another level it is a real means of deception. If everything the devil did always appeared obviously bad, we would all avoid him like the plague. But he does not work like that. One of the main ways the devil works is to take what is good and entirely of God, and then pervert it slightly so that instead of leading us to God, it leads us away from him, the true originator. Often the devil appears extremely attractive. The suggestions he puts to us appear to make good sense and, even more importantly, when we follow them, the results can seem absolutely marvellous at first. Again, if there were total disaster every time we followed one of the devil's suggestions, we would all be one hundred per cent safe, because we would know. But the devil does not work like that. He is not as powerful as we sometimes make him appear, but neither is he stupid; and he is just as capable of giving what appear to be 'gifts' as God, in order to secure his own ends. Especially in the early days where he is trying to ensnare us, he is quick to pour out apparent gifts—for instance, apparent healing through the use of crystals, or enhanced spiritual power through meditation. The last thing the devil wants at this point is for there to be problems. In fact, he will try very hard to ensure that they do not occur. His gifts, however, are illusions and are ultimately incapable of building us up. They do not give a real feeling of wholeness because they are power-based.

In these circumstances God may well allow problems to manifest simply to expose what is actually going on. To put it another way, he may even send a spirit/angel with the express charge of precipitating a crisis, so as to expose the deception at work and frustrate whatever short- or long-term plans the devil might have in mind. We must make no mistake, there is a real war here, and sufferings, problems and difficulties in this kind of situation are not coming from the devil, although they arise only because of the hold the devil has over us. God permits them—sends them if you like—in order to win us back to himself.

We tend to categorise all spirits who precipitate any kind of perceived harm as evil, but the teaching of the Bible and early non-canonical Hebrew tradition is rather different. In Scripture, God uses his servants in the spiritual realm in ways that will best recall us to himself and facilitate our ultimate healing. Hebrew traditions, however, go even further and are quite explicit. A clear distinction is drawn between those angelic beings or spirits who have rebelled against God, and those who have remained faithful, but both remain very firmly under God's sovereignty and serve his purposes (for further discussion on this point see Chapter 9). It would appear that on occasion God permits angels in rebellion against himself and hostile to mankind to test men and women in order to prove their faith (see Job 1–2), but non-canonical traditions also specifically refer to angelic beings who have apparently never wavered in their obedience to God, and who implement his commands for judgement (it would appear to be just such an angel who implements God's anger against Israel in 2 Samuel 24:17). In the non-canonical traditions such angels are sometimes referred to as evil, but it seems that their apparent hostility towards men and women arises simply because of our rebellion against God. They are then to be clearly distinguished from those angelic beings who are themselves in rebellion against God and more properly to be seen as 'evil'.

We have already seen how God 'tests' his children in order to educate and teach (Chapter 2 above). In the same way, God will not allow evil to maintain dominion over us, and the effects of his fierce love may appear dire. But the point is, God's will is ultimately to save and not to harm. He never coerces or forces our compliance. Rather, he leaves the choice with us. To call the spirits who implement his will here 'evil' is, I believe, a misnomer, because they serve God's purposes for redemption—but while we are in rebellion they are set implacably against us.

This therefore points to the fundamental difference between those spirits who serve the purposes of God in obedience, and those who give allegiance to the devil. The devil tries to destroy, but God seeks to redeem. The devil coerces and will do all in his power to fetter the free exercise of our will, but God always maintains respect for the choices *we* make and never attempts to dominate. The devil will not let go without a struggle, but God rejoices and showers us with love when we turn back to him.

What happens may sometimes appear harsh—indeed the Old Testament picture is harsh—but Jesus demonstrates to us a truth that goes far beyond that. He shows us, by his life and teaching, that God is love, and that he wills for us only what is good. God's will is never to cause harm, but he will not compromise with evil—and he will not allow it to continue to work away underground. In this situation, he will expose it.

The devil only moves obviously to attack once we respond to God. At that point he will mobilise every weapon in his arsenal in order to try and prevent us from coming back to God—and if we thought we had problems before, then it can seem that they really escalate at this point, because the hold the devil has on us enables him to have a grip on our lives, and a real battle for our soul begins. When we begin to follow him, the last thing the devil wants is for us to have difficulties. At this point he will give us all sorts of apparent gifts, and some of them will appear extremely desirable and will give to us feelings of being 'special' or 'chosen', and better than others, because we shall believe we have some kind of power. The deeper we get embroiled, the greater the hold the devil will have over our lives, and not just over our lives, but over the lives of those we love, and over our children and our descendants too.

Recently, a girl called Mary was referred to us for ministry because she was being 'haunted' by a dead friend. Some two years previously, a young man who had been a part of the crowd she was in, had died very suddenly of a brain haemorrhage. Ever since the funeral she had had an increasing sense of his presence, to the extent that at times she had felt him to be physically there. The situation took a new turn, however, when she began receiving messages from him through automatic writing, telling her to do certain things or contact certain people. She was not a Christian when all this started and initially she had been very excited, telling all her friends. They too had responded with enthusiasm, but then she had begun to feel frightened, and it was at this point that through a friend she was put in touch with us. She was absolutely convinced that the experiences she was having were genuine. She showed us examples of the messages, and related one particular instance that had spectacularly been proved true. She had been asked, with incredible urgency and late at night, to contact the dead boy's mother. When she had unwillingly done so, she had discovered that the lady had been on the point of committing suicide, and it was only Mary's intervention that pulled her back. Pretty dramatic, but now she was scared.

The crowd she mixed with were into drugs and all sorts of semi-Eastern ideas, such as reincarnation and meditation. I believe that what had happened was that through all this, she had opened herself up to spiritual forces that were not from God. These experiences had at first been tremendously exciting, and had seemed positive. They had given her a real feeling of being of use and important, but at the same time they had been an intrusion into the most private places of her spirit.

Nothing obviously bad had happened to her at all, because the devil was giving her apparently 'good' things as he sought to gain a hold. Her feelings of fear here, I believe, were healthy and came straight from the Lord.

This kind of thing can be dealt with only by God. We cannot close this kind of access, once it has been opened, by ourselves, although we can try to repress it. The only way to deal with it, finally, is to repent, and ask the Lord himself to come and sever the hold. A word of warning, however. This kind of prayer should never be undertaken lightly, nor without prayer cover from others, both for those ministering and for the one receiving ministry. The spiritual forces we are dealing with are very real—and of course the point also needs to be made (even though it should be obvious) that *we* are not dealing with them at all, but God. I believe that this kind of ministry should *never* be undertaken unless the Lord himself calls us to it.

What happened with Mary was that I met and prayed with her with another member from our ministry team, and she asked the Lord into her life. We then asked for the Spirit to come upon her, and at this point the Lord simply took over. While we quietly prayed with her for about half an hour, the Spirit wrapped her (it's the only way of describing it), purifying and healing her, and sealing up the access point to her life. It is a pretty dramatic way of coming to know the Lord, but it underlines the point that the workings of the devil, at least at first, are not always obviously bad . . . and not all problems encountered come from him.

5
Jesus and the Devil

There are people today (and some of them Christians) who see evil as having overwhelming power and control—just as in the same way there are others who deny the existence of evil, or who even claim that it is a part of God. Both positions are not only wrong, but dangerous. To gain understanding we have to turn to the gospels, because it is only here—in his confrontation with Jesus—that we have the full character of the devil unmasked, and the nature of the conflict exposed.

Battle is joined

If the devil has been in the background throughout the Old Testament, a very different picture emerges with the coming of Christ. Up to this time, there have been many promises of redemption and restoration for the state of Israel, and there is undeniably a strong consciousness of the supernatural throughout the early writings, but there has not been any real indication of the enormous spiritual powers pitted against the rule of God. The Jews have been rebellious and have turned to other gods, true, but the idea of some organising and focused force behind these powers has been absent.

Now, however, the mask is ripped away and from the very beginning there is a real consciousness of conflict and of battle having been joined.

The opening verses of John proclaim:

> In the beginning was the Word, and the Word was with God, and the Word was God. He was with God in the beginning.
>
> Through him all things were made; without him nothing was made that has been made. In him was life, and that life was the light of men. The light shines in the darkness, but the darkness has not understood it . . . He was in the world, and though the world was made through him, the world did not recognise him. He came to that which was his own, but his own did not receive him. Yet to all who received him, to those who believed in his name, he gave the right to become children of God (John 1:1–5, 10–12).

These words are crucial to our understanding, because they tell us some important facts about the devil. First, they categorically state that God brought into being the *whole of creation* through his Word. That means not just men and women and the whole of the material world around us, including the galaxies, but all spiritual powers and beings as well. Everything that exists, including the devil, owes its existence to God, which makes the devil inferior to God. Not only does the devil simply not have the creative powers of God but, more than that, he is dependent on him for his own existence.

Now the devil tries to make us believe a very different picture. He attempts to convince us that he is equal to, or even greater in power than, God—and so to divert the worship that rightfully belongs to God to himself. We have seen from the rabbinic traditions referred to in

Isaiah 14:13–14 and Ezekiel 28:12–19 that, as Lucifer, he rebelled against God and tried to seize the rule of heaven for himself, and that he drew a number of other angels around himself in that rebellion. But he cannot get away from this one basic fact: he was made and had a beginning—whereas God simply *is*. God is sovereign.

Second, these words tell us that there is conflict, and that this conflict exists on a cosmic scale, with the devil being portrayed as the darkness that has blinded mankind to the true light of God. What this means for each one of us personally is that at every level of life, when we are not submitted to the lordship of Christ, there is a real struggle going on. It does not mean that we automatically belong to the devil, but without that obedience to God which ensures our protection we are fair game—up for grabs—and we will be attacked. And because we are limited and flawed, there will be times when we succumb, and each time we do that the devil's hold over us will be intensified.

This awareness of conflict with evil does not only come from the 'theological bits' within the gospels; that is, the parts where the evangelists reflect on the spiritual truths and insights they have gained through witnessing Jesus' life and death. It comes also from the words and conduct of Jesus himself. Right at the beginning of his ministry, the Lord announces that he has come to usher in the kingdom of God and set free those who are in any kind of captivity (eg, Matthew 4:17; Mark 1:14–15; Luke 4:18–21). It is a message that echoes and re-echoes throughout Jesus' teaching, combined with an insistence on the necessity for all of us now to make a choice—to decide which side we are on before it is too late. Also, and perhaps most tellingly, the conduct of Jesus' ministry is itself surrounded with conflict.

Faced by the obvious power that surrounds and pours from Jesus, the devil is from the beginning forced out into the open and his pretensions exposed. This, we know, is not the way the devil likes to work, because his operations up to this time have been covert. But if he is to try now and counter the power of God, he has to engage in far more blatant aggression. The devil does not choose the ground of battle; he can only respond. Left to himself, he would surely have preferred things to remain unchanged, while he just carried on consolidating his power.

There is perhaps a lesson here for all of us today, because it is as the power of God is felt that the works of the devil *are* forced out into the open. People often say that when a church begins to experience revival there is an escalation in demonic activity, but that is only partly true. Certainly the devil responds as God moves (and we shall examine this in relation to Jesus' birth below), but it is equally true that it is God's light simply revealing what has been in place all the time, so that the devil is no longer able to hide.

Here then in the gospels, for the first time, battle is openly joined, and a very different picture emerges from the one we have in the Old Testament. If John sets the scene, Matthew and Luke chart the onset of hostilities from before even the moment of Jesus' birth. We learn from Luke, for example, that Mary has to travel by donkey to Bethlehem for the census—a journey hardly to be recommended for someone about to give birth. Luke tells us that this has been brought about by God to fulfil the prophecy that the Christ would be born in Bethlehem of Judea. But while we see God's mighty hand here and the angels rejoice, at the same time—from Matthew's account—we are aware of evil reaching out like a net to entrap and destroy the incarnate Son of God before he can grow to manhood and become in actuality the threat Satan knows him to be.

It reads almost like a complicated game of chess, but at every point it is God who is sovereign and controlling the situation. The Magi, for example, stop off in Jerusalem and Herod is alerted, but God intervenes and warns them in a dream so that they do not return as requested, and tell the king where the young child is.

Round One to God. But Satan is clearly not ready simply to acknowledge defeat, and so the campaign continues. Surely it is under the devil's malign influence that Herod gives the command for all male children in the region under the age of two to be slaughtered (Matthew 2:16–18)? Yet even this is too late, because God has already removed Mary and Joseph and the child to safety in Egypt.

From the moment of conception, then, it seems that Satan lies in wait for Jesus, determined to devour him. As an angelic being, even if fallen, he would appear to know that the ruler of the world is coming. But he is not omniscient. He can see neither the exact time nor the place. God protects Mary. He shrouds her with his Spirit like a cloak. He sends angels to warn her and Joseph and, despite the intensity of the attack launched by the devil, he leads them to safety. Yet not without cost.

I have always felt that the slaughter of the innocents could be likened to a demonic version of saturation bombing. Satan knows what is at stake, and he blitzes the entire area. From the text in Matthew we know that he causes devastation, and yet, interestingly, God does not intervene. Should we infer from this that God does not care? Of course not, but I think it tells us something of the intensity and the sheer deadliness of the conflict of which we are ourselves a part.

However, quite apart from the fact that these early scenes show the devil gearing up for war, we gain some important insights into how he operates. We see, for example, that the devil works through human agency, just as much as God does. In the devil's case, at the time of Jesus' birth, his agent is Herod, the king.

The text does not specifically state that Herod is a tool of the devil, of course, but from his paranoia when first hearing the news, the deviousness of his attempts to use the Magi, and his overwhelming fury on learning he has been duped, he is clearly being manipulated by forces beyond himself. At a purely worldly level, of course, Herod's emotions can be justified. He is a foreigner (a Jew of Idumaean descent) and not the rightful King of Israel. The birth of a child of the line of David, and fulfilling all the prophecies of a Davidic king who would lead his people to freedom, could well have been seen by him as posing a major threat. And, like many worldly monarchs, he is ruthless in maintaining his position. Evil, however, *is* clearly at work—shown not just by Herod's underhand and devious attempts to discover the birthplace of his supposed rival, but in his bizarre order to slaughter all male children under two. In other words, the devil appeals to Herod's desire to maintain his own position and implants in his mind a way of ensuring this. But does this mean that the king is possessed? We shall return to this question later.

The point to be made here is that although the devil is not omniscient in the same way as God, he clearly does have foresight and he is aware of the scale of the threat being posed. Yet he has no precise knowledge of Jesus' birth before the alert is provided by the wise men, and he cannot immediately locate the child, even once that alert has been given. His foresight is limited, and it is this that forces him to act in a way that is perhaps far more open than he would like. It is this that forces him to reveal himself, and his method of attack is brilliant—through Herod the foreigner king. We can see from this that the devil works through both people and institutions.

The second point is also clear. The devil will stop at nothing to exterminate goodness and thwart the plans of God. Looked at rationally, he was way over the top in his response, but he knew what God was doing, and he was determined to stamp it out before it could become a threat. In the same way, I think, the devil knows who God plans to use today and so he harries and literally bedevils them—sometimes even before they have come to know God. He is attempting, of course, by unremitting attack, hardship and the implanting of self-doubt, to disable and discourage them so that they will be prevented from ever coming to the point of hearing God's will for their lives. And I believe the more the Lord wishes to use people, the stronger that attack can be. Not always, of course, but I have seen this scenario repeated too often to doubt that it happens. Sometimes it can seem that people lurch from disaster to disaster, and absolutely nothing goes right, although all too often it seems due to circumstances entirely beyond the individual's control.

Yet although this kind of harrying is demonic in origin, it cannot happen without the Lord's permission. This does not mean that God wills this hardship or pain, but he permits it in order to discipline and build us up. As Jesus himself said, temptations have to come

(Luke 17:1). What matters is our response and attitude—that is the determiner of whether we grow in grace and freedom, or whether we become bound and twisted by Satan. Where God has a work ahead for us, the training is correspondingly rigorous—and God permits the devil this kind of access so that we might grow in strength. Sometimes that suffering actually brings us to the Lord, and sometimes it is through the pain that we learn the reality of Christ's victory as something for ourselves. It is when we have really learned the truth of that victory—and move in the assurance of that victory—that God can use us to help others.

So if, as you read this, you are going through a time of intense pain and even loneliness, and God feels a million miles away—take heart, he has not abandoned you. God is there in the darkest place, and if we just cling to him, he always brings us through. As we see with Jesus himself, the dawning of the Day of the Lord starts in terrible darkness, but at no point is God ever out of control. If we never see the immensity of God's care, and the real power of his victory for ourselves, how can we know it is really there?

A further point needs to be made here before we move on to examine Jesus' personal perception of the devil. Where this kind of hardship is experienced, it is not the result of judgement, even though suffering might be allowed as a result of unacknowledged sin in our lives, which needs repentance and cleansing in order for the hold to be broken. Again, this is something that we are all in danger of sometimes assuming, but the Bible teaches us that actual judgement is reserved for a later time, and is dependent upon our response to God made in this life. For the period of this life all of God's permissions and actions are to recall us to himself, and to bring us to life. The devil knows this.

To sum up this section, Satan's sphere of operations is confined to this world, although as a spiritual being he exists outside of and beyond the material. He has his minions in the spiritual realms, as attested to by Scripture (see Chapter 10), and they are undeniably powerful. But it would appear too that they can only operate within this world and that men and women are only vulnerable to ensnarement by them for the period of their lives upon earth. For men and women, the important thing is whether or not we succumb to the devil's wiles and (whether consciously or not) choose for him and against God. If we do this and reject God, then we do fall under judgement—God's judgement—in which case we shall be subject to the same punishment as Lucifer himself and consigned to the same place of confinement after death (see Revelation 20:7–15).

The devil then does not himself hold the power of final destruction, although—yet again—he would like to fool us into believing that he does. Nevertheless, as has already been said, it must be recognised that for the period of this life there are casualties—and the mass slaughter of the babies in Bethlehem tragically illustrates this. Satan held no final power over those innocent children—they remained in God's hand—but he could and did engineer their deaths. And God permitted that, because to have done otherwise would have been to intervene at a spiritual level in human sin in a way that would have restricted human choice. Herod chose to listen to the promptings of the devil. His actions were evil, but he chose to make that response—he chose *for* Satan and *against* God and, for this life, God would not override that choice.

So, we can see that the conflict is both real and directed—but what did Jesus himself think?

Jesus' perception of the devil

Despite what some people would like to believe, Jesus did not think the devil was a figment of the imagination. From the beginning, his ministry brought him into open conflict with Satan, but at the same time his perception was that his call from God was far broader. He came proclaiming that the kingdom of God—the rule of God—was not only near, but was beginning in him. He came to tell the poor the good news; to set free those who were bound up—by whatever circumstances; to restore sight to blind eyes; and to release those who were bowed down and oppressed (see Luke 4:18–19). He came to baptise with the Holy Spirit (John 1:32–34).

For Jesus, inevitably, this involved breaking the stranglehold which the devil had so effectively maintained down the centuries—ever since, in fact, Adam and Eve had first succumbed to temptation and opened up the great barrier between themselves and God. So, we can see he took Satan very seriously, and to suggest that Jesus' worldview was simply the product of first-century knowledge and superstitiously inclined cultural conditioning is not only patronising, but denies God the capacity to have taken that into account and to have transcended the problem—if problem it was. It also denies the character of Jesus himself, because at no point in the gospels do we see a man who simply accepted without question the prevailing ideas and attitudes of his day, whether it brought him into a head-on clash with the religious authorities (eg, Luke

6:1–11; Matthew 12:1–14; Mark 2:23–28) or whether it overturned the social conventions and moral attitudes of his day (eg, John 8:3–11). Jesus was in every sense a radical—and he had his own clear ideas of God's truth, which he was not afraid to proclaim.

But Jesus did not focus upon the devil. Jesus focused upon, and was obedient to, his Father, God. The devil was simply the adversary—the oppressor—who had done so much to block the Father's will and had bound up God's children in ways from which they were unable to break free . . . unless God himself intervened.

Interestingly, the names Jesus assigns Satan, and his descriptions of him, are wholly in line with, and confirm, the earlier rabbinic traditions of the nature and origins of the devil. Jesus, for instance, calls Satan the 'prince of this world' (John 14: 30), suggesting an original legitimate authority conferred by God. And in Luke 10:18 he says, 'I saw Satan fall like lightning from heaven.' This verse has always excited controversy, but the view which sees it as a prophetic utterance indicating final judgement remains unconvincing. Taken in conjunction with Isaiah 14:12, however, it can be far more convincingly interpreted as an eye-witness report of the rebellion in heaven for which Satan, as leader, was cast down. In effect, then, Jesus is saying here that as Son of God, he was there when Satan was thrown down to earth.

To Jesus, the devil was the ruler of this age, with his own disciples and power network in place. But at the same time he remained simply an upstart angelic being who had rebelled against God and was now wielding legitimate power in an illegitimate way. A force to be reckoned with, true, but at no point even remotely equal in stature to God. As Jesus appears to have seen it, God's rule had been challenged by this usurper prince who now had to be dealt with. He knew that there was real power here and that it was not going to be easy, but at the same time he knew that while he remained obedient, the outcome was certain. He said this clearly to the disciples: 'I have told you now before it happens, so that when it does happen you will believe. I will not speak with you much longer, for the prince of this world is coming. He has no hold on me, but the world must learn that I love the Father and that I do exactly what my Father has commanded me' (John 14:29–31).

Jesus' actions and teaching throughout his ministry were entirely consistent with this view. From the moment of his own baptism he proclaimed the inbreaking power of God, healing people *and* regularly exorcising demons. However, it is important to note that Jesus did *not* attribute all sickness to the presence of demons. In John 5:14, for example, he specifically tells the lame man who has been healed at the pool of Bethesda, 'Stop sinning or something worse may happen to you.' There is no suggestion of deliverance from an evil spirit, but physical bondage has clearly arisen as a result of sin. It is an important and frequently ignored distinction.

On the other hand, in Luke 13:1–5, Jesus says that the tragedy that has overtaken the executed Galileans, and the eighteen who have been crushed to death by the collapse of a tower at Siloam, was due neither to demonic activity nor to sin. People often comment that all suffering is a result of the Fall, and clearly this is true, but it would appear from Jesus' words that not *all* suffering is a result of specific targeting. That is, Jesus' words would suggest that in some (albeit not widespread) circumstances, there is an element of random chance operative. Suffering in general is a result of the Fall, but it is simply not right to see all problems exclusively in terms of 'cause and effect'. That some problems do arise from sin or demonic hold is undeniable, yet equally we can become the object of demonic attack where there is no legal 'cause', but rather because the Devil is reacting adversely to the activities and intentions of the Holy Spirit working through us.

Where overt demonic activity was present, Jesus neither played around nor entered into lengthy theological debate. Rather, he simply addressed the spirit and commanded it to go (eg, Luke 4:40–41). We can see then that he drew a distinction between situations where someone had been bound up by Satan—in which case he forgave the sin and released them from the devil's hold—and cases where demons had entered in, and had to be expelled. It would seem that sin, while opening up the way to satanic bondage, does not automatically allow the entry of demons, and that the situations have to be carefully distinguished (see Chapter 10).

From the gospels we see that where demons are present, except where commanded to be silent, they are often extremely vocal—and all of them, without exception, recognise Jesus for who he is. That is, they recognise the power and presence of God, even though that knowledge is at the time hidden from men and women. In fact the first real confession of faith in the gospel narratives, discounting the witness of Simeon (Luke 2:30–32) is from a demon (Luke 4:34)! We shall look at this further in Chapter 10, but it is important here to note the words of the demons. Often they ask Jesus if he has come to destroy or torture them, but they also display awareness that a time for their destruction has already been fixed. In the account of the healing of the two demon-possessed men in Matthew 8, the demons say to Jesus, 'Have you come here to torture us *before the appointed time*?' (italics mine).

So, both Jesus and the demons would appear to know that the latter are only going to be allowed to operate for a fixed time, and that the writing is already on the wall. The demons know that God is greater, and that they have to give way. Whatever contrary impression Satan tries to give (cf. Matthew 4:1-11; Mark 1:12-13; Luke 4:1-13), they seem to know that they are defeated even before Jesus comes, and they certainly know they cannot stand in his presence. At the same time, until the day fixed for final judgement arrives—when they and their lord will be dealt with—they appear to expect to be allowed to continue their activities.

Jesus, then, distinguishes between demons and their lord. The demons have to give way before him, and he would appear to acknowledge their comments on final judgement. But for him the real confrontation and contest is undoubtedly with Satan.

Like the demons, Satan recognises Jesus, but he does not so easily acknowledge the latter's power. He remains in fact the rebellious and proud angel, and it is his power and hold that Jesus finally breaks on the cross. Even before Jesus died, the demons could not stand before him. Satan, their lord, apparently could, but on the cross Jesus once and for all defeated him too.

Today demons still recognise and tremble before the power of Christ. If they knew then, they know with even more certainty now that they are defeated. They cannot remain in the presence of God. Jesus irrevocably broke Satan's hold over the earth by his death on the cross. At the same time he said clearly that the fixed time for final judgement had still not yet arrived, but lay in the future (eg, Mark 13:1–37; Matthew 24:1–51; Luke 21:5–36). When judgement does come, the demons know that along with Satan and men and women who have not acknowledged God's rule, they will be consigned by God to the place of eternal punishment.

6

The Devil's Strategy

We have already seen that the devil worked extremely hard to try to prevent Jesus from ever beginning his ministry. However, for all his foreknowledge, he had no precise knowledge of Jesus' location . . . until, that is, Jesus was revealed by the powerful anointing of the Spirit. After this, his presence could no longer be concealed.

People often comment with surprise on what appears from the gospel accounts to be the huge escalation in demonic activity at around the time of Jesus' birth and for the period of his life. I do not believe that this was an accident. Neither do I believe that the style used to report Jesus' ministry can be attributed solely to a growing sense of apocalypticism, which led to an unprecedented highlighting of what were really fairly commonplace events. (Apocalypticism looked to the dawning of a new age of salvation, ushered in as a direct result of divine intervention, and framed in a visionary, highly symbolic style that reinterpreted and applied the prophetic promises of restoration . . . but which often did not seem to have much grounding in reality.)

We need to recap a little here. The devil is nowhere

near so overt in his actions in the Old Testament as he appears to be in the New. Against this, it remains true that for the Jews of the earliest centuries, struggling to maintain and give form to the monotheistic belief that had been revealed to them, to have given such emphasis to a power that was other than God would have been unthinkable. They just would not have used this kind of language, because to have done so would have come perilously near to suggesting, if not two gods, at least a major spiritual power that *could* and *would* take on God. This would have been totally unacceptable.

However, it would also seem to be true that there simply was not such a high level of *manifest* demonic activity before Jesus appeared on the scene. People became sick, yes, and dabbled in things they should not have dabbled in (Saul is a good example of this), but there simply was not the same level of demonic possession and confrontation that appears to have erupted when Jesus revealed himself.

So, exactly what was going on here? Why should this have happened? Three questions in particular arise. First, was the devil stepping up his attack because he knew the final showdown was about to take place? Second, had he grown in power over the centuries so that he could now act in this supremely blatant way? Or, third, as noted before, was it that the coming of Jesus in such power forced him to come out into the open in a way that was in fact intensely uncomfortable, and not at all what he wanted? I suggest that the answer to all three questions is 'yes'.

The devil was stepping up his attack because he had, as he thought, usurped the position of God. He was the ruler of this world (Jesus himself acknowledged him as this). He wanted to make that hold complete. He was setting himself up as a rival god, and as justification he could point to the high level of support he had received down the centuries from people the world over.

Second, the devil's hold had grown stronger since that first fall from grace by Adam and Eve because, by giving him the worship he craved, people had effectively wound themselves even further into his grip. They had come to a point now where they belonged to him! He owned them, and there was no way he was going to let go. So he could be more overt in his actions, simply because the net he had cast was drawing tight, and they were all (as he thought) safely inside. But the devil had reckoned without the irresistible power of God, and that brings us to the third point.

The devil likes to work in secret. Even today, he far prefers guerrilla tactics to war waged out in the open, where he will be exposed and might well get beaten. He is not stupid, and he by no means has the total control over our lives and events that he would like to fool us into believing he has. He knows perfectly well, for instance, that if he prematurely reveals himself, we shall be so horrified that we shall dig our heels in and say 'no'. Because at the end of the day we do still have free will—that is one of God's gifts that he cannot take away for the period of this life, although he can interfere with and influence it, and so get a hold over us. Basically, however, the devil does not like to be exposed, and he is not too keen on having his hold on people on show either. And yet, as Jesus sets out on his ministry we find demons erupting on all sides, and all, as often as not, screaming out, 'You are the Son of God!' (eg, Luke 4:33–35, 41f., etc). They cannot help themselves. They recognise Jesus, and the power that flows out of him leaves them no place to hide. They are forced into the open, and then Jesus deals with them. As we have seen, he does not enter into any long chats or theological arguments, or ask them what they are doing there; he simply tells them to be quiet and go. We see this, for example, in Jesus' healing of the demon-possessed man who dwelt among the tombs: 'When he saw Jesus from a distance, he ran and fell on his knees in front of him. He shouted at the top of his voice, "What do you want with me, Jesus, Son of the Most High God? Swear to God that you won't torture me!" For Jesus had said to him, "Come out of this man, you evil spirit!"' (Mark 5:6–20).

This is not just an interesting insight into Jesus' ministry, but actually has important implications for our own ministry today. A church that has not been empowered by the Holy Spirit is often a very orderly and well-mannered church, at least on the surface. But let the Spirit start to move and all sorts of odd and amazing things will happen, and some of them will unquestionably be demonic. Similarly, in our own lives, when we grow closer to God and he really begins to use us, there is not uncommonly what seems to be a real outbreak of demonic power, manifesting in a whole range of bizarre problems.

I was recently involved in ministry to a lady who was a stalwart of her local church. She had done a tremendous amount of children's work, and whenever any catering was needed for church events she was there! She had always, however, distanced herself from anything even remotely 'religious'. Then one day, after a particularly moving service, she asked someone to pray with her . . . and all hell broke loose. In the month that followed, at a practical level, she seemed to fall apart as something in her fought with God—it was the only way to describe it. She was unable to concentrate on anything and during that time she even had a minor car accident. Something seemed to have 'taken over', she said. At the end of that period, after six hours of solid prayer, she was delivered from a spirit that had been strangling every spiritual step she took since early childhood. I have to say that it was a horrendous month, but her joy and peace after that time were absolutely amazing. Everyone said she was a changed lady.

It needs to be stressed that when this sort of thing begins to happen, it is not actually anything new being exposed, but rather whatever hold or damage was already there. When God permits that, he will deal with it. However, if people do not understand what is happening, they are often tempted at this point to give up (which is just what the devil wants). It cannot be stressed too strongly that to do that is disastrous because it leads to the devil's hold being strengthened—by our own demoralisation. This kind of encounter is a battle, and the only thing to do is to persevere and go forward. Above all, we need to be able to recognise when this kind of attack is taking place. Nowhere do we see this method of attack more clearly delineated than in the campaign the devil waged against Jesus.

The devil's attack on Jesus

We have seen how the devil attempted to destroy Jesus at birth, and failed. As Jesus grew, we know that God hid his Son. But once Jesus had been baptised by the indwelling power of the Spirit, that was no longer possible. From that point Jesus stood out like a beacon on a hill, and that meant that he became subject to the full weight of attack. That he was sinless did not mean that the devil could not attack him. In fact, it meant the reverse, because his very sinlessness focused the devil's gaze. And we know that Jesus suffered under this attack.

Once he had Jesus in his sights, the devil adopted a policy which incorporated four different lines of attack.

1. Temptation

From the very beginning of his ministry Jesus was subject to temptation (eg, Matthew 4:1–11; Luke 4:1–13; Mark 1:12–13), and we know that this continued right up until the moment of his death (Matthew 27:40). Interestingly, the temptations were rarely to direct disobedience to God, which would perhaps have been easier to counter (cf. Matthew 16:21–23), but rather to reliance, for the fulfilment of his ministry, on things that in themselves might have seemed good, but which led away from the path God had set before him.

The three wilderness temptations are an excellent example of this and tell us much. Each suggestion would appear, on the face of it, eminently justifiable. Take the first temptation. 'You're hungry!' says the devil. 'Turn the stones to bread!' At a very basic level, what could be more reasonable? Jesus was hungry—so why not use some of his miraculous powers to satisfy his perfectly natural bodily needs? But the temptation is subtler than that, because in effect Satan is saying, 'Use the powers you *rightly* have to draw people after you and prove you're the Son of God!' But to have succumbed to that, while it might have been an easy way of attracting attention and even worship, and would certainly have by-passed the need to die, would simply have substituted domination by Satan for that of Jesus. People need never have wanted again. Of course they would have followed Jesus. But God wanted the world to be set free; he did not just want one form of domination swapped for another.

While perhaps not many of us will be tempted to achieve our ends by a wrong use of the spectacular, we can all be tempted by the lure of status and the enhancement of our own reputation, and we can all want the instant fulfilment of our material needs. In fact, on all counts this first temptation seems peculiarly relevant to us today and maybe all of us need to learn from Jesus' response: first, that our service of God should never lead to a focusing of attention on ourselves (this is how cults begin) and, second, that obedience to God does not automatically and necessarily entail the instant satisfaction of all our natural desires. It is a temptation to which all of us, to a greater or lesser degree, fall prey—especially in the evangelical wing of the church. But we need to learn that obedience to God can sometimes mean a little bit of discomfort—a little bit of want. It can even sometimes mean being in a place we would prefer not to be!

Similarly, when the devil took Jesus and showed him all the kingdoms of the world in a moment of time and said, 'You can have the lot! All you need do is worship me!' What could have been more reasonable? Jesus had come into the world to re-establish God's sovereignty and rule, and the devil said, 'Okay! I'll co-operate. Look, all the structures are in place. I'll give you carte blanche. You'll be the ruler. All you have to do is worship me!'

The temptation actually was for Jesus to become an idol, and he could have done it easily . . . if he had only played the world's game and turned his back on God. What a victory for Satan that would have been. The whole world focused on Jesus, and Jesus focused on him! But why not? Jesus would have done what God wanted, established his messianic rule!

How many of us today, I wonder, hear a variation of that temptation? Go along with the rules the world lays down, and you'll have it all—status, authority, two holidays a year . . . peace. It was the same temptation to which Herod succumbed, and to which we are all sometimes subjected. How often, I wonder, does it creep even into the church itself? For this is not simply the temptation to worldly position and goods—it includes also ideas and attitudes. In fact, it seems particularly relevant today when we think of the plethora of New Age ideas and philosophies that in every sense 'promise us the world', but lead away from God.

Finally, of course the devil takes Jesus to the highest pinnacle of the temple in Jerusalem and invites him to throw himself down, on the grounds that the angels will all rush to his aid. He supports this suggestion with a quotation from Psalm 91:11–12 which affirms that those who trust in the Lord will be assured of his protection. What we have here, of course, is not so much a deceitful use of Scripture, as a subtle misapplication which might easily, if applied without due reverence, lead to sin. And the devil can and does quote Scripture—even today.

Some see this last suggestion as a temptation to self-advertisement, but more subtly it is a temptation to try to test God. We can all sometimes do this if we are not careful. It is the demand put upon God for him to demonstrate his power. 'You're God,' we say, 'so do this! Heal this person! Give him back his sight! Make her walk!' It is the demand *we* make, as opposed to our obedient response, and it is not always easy to see the abyss that yawns between.

Jesus retaliates by his own quotation, 'Do not put the Lord your God to the test' (Deuteronomy 6:16). He recognises that to *demand* miraculous protection as 'proof' of God's love and care is wrong. It is the seeking after a sign that elsewhere he condemns so vehemently (eg, Matthew 12:39f.). Rather, the right attitude, he says, is simply to trust and obey. *Anything* beyond that comes from sin.

All of these are, of course, attacks upon the mind. This is a form of temptation the devil is very fond of, and it can be extremely difficult both to discern and combat. Our only defence is to stay close to God.

2. *Doubt*

The second line of attack the devil employed was through the medium of others. Time and again he attempted to erode Jesus' confidence and fill his mind with self-doubt through the comments and actions of others, especially those closest to him.

Throughout his ministry Jesus had to contend with hostility and accusations of heresy from the religious authorities of the day. It got so bad that on occasion the Pharisees even accused him of being empowered by Satan (eg, Matthew 12:24: 'It is only by Beelzebub, the prince of demons, that this fellow drives out demons'; cf. Luke 11:15; Mark 3:22). But how much more wounding must have been the incredulity and doubt on the part of his family and, at times, his friends? In Mark, for example, we read that when his family apparently first heard about the spectacle he was making of himself, they set out to 'take charge of him', because they imagined that he had gone mad (Mark 3:21).

A favourite strategy of the devil is to implant doubt and confusion. In particular, the devil likes to undermine relationships and sow mistrust. All too clearly, this was what he attempted to do with Jesus. But even more damaging than the mistrust of others is mistrust of oneself; and the pressure put upon Jesus to doubt himself in face of the evident disbelief of his mother and brothers (or, at the least, to have been more restrained) must have been tremendous. Rightly Jesus resisted this, but again this would have been a powerful attack on his mind.

Subtle attack came too through the misunderstanding *concern* of his friends—that is, the apostles. Throughout his ministry Jesus patiently prepared the apostles for the work that lay ahead of them. Unquestionably there were periods of excitement and certainty, for example, when Peter for the first time said openly to Jesus, 'You are the Christ' (Mark 8:27–30; Matthew 16:13–16; Luke 9:18–20). But there were also times of doubt and discouragement, when the disciples found certain things that Jesus said hard to bear, impossible even. We see this perhaps most clearly in the incident just referred to above with Peter because, having given voice to the marvellous certainty that Jesus *was* the long-awaited Christ, the next minute Peter was trying to persuade Jesus that he was being unduly pessimistic in predicting the suffering and death that lay ahead of him in Jerusalem. Again, this was a temptation for Jesus to deviate from the path God had set before him, and he instantly recognised it for what it was. Almost ignoring Peter, he directly addressed Satan, whose mouthpiece the apostle had temporarily become. 'Get behind me, Satan! . . . You do not have in mind the things of God, but the things of men' (Mark 8:33).

This must have been devastating for Peter, but it serves to show the ease with which the devil can interfere with our thoughts and implant unhelpful suggestions, even when we are in no way submitted to his lordship. Here Peter was actually vulnerable because of his love. He succumbed because he still had so much to learn about obedience and trust and the character of God. In a nutshell, he made a mistake, as we all inevitably do, but the result was that the devil immediately leapt in and took advantage, and Jesus recognised instantly what was going on. It is sometimes said that Jesus was too harsh here, but actually the way he responded only served to show how great a threat he thought was being posed. He knew that this was serious. The words would affect those who heard and might even, if not rebuked, gnaw away at him too. It had to be dealt with. The nature of his response, far from being harsh, serves merely to illustrate the seriousness with which Jesus regarded Satan, and his perception of the nature of the struggle.

3. Criticism and accusation

As already mentioned, throughout his ministry Jesus had to contend with hostility and accusations of heresy from the religious authorities. Some of the latter comments would have arisen from a genuine lack of comprehension on the part of those around him and are understandable, even commendable (eg, John 3:1–10). But there is a world of difference between words expressing lack of understanding (or even rebuke) where the words spring from a basic openness and there is real desire to follow God—and words borne of a desire to maintain the status quo, which will not admit of change for fear of jeopardising one's own position or damaging 'the way things are' . . . whatever God might be saying.

The religious authorities constantly opposed Jesus, even in face of the signs and wonders that confirmed his ministry, because to have acknowledged his status would have shaken to the core the foundations of their religious belief and practice. They paid lip-service to God, and were careful to maintain all the outward forms of religious observance, but basically their hearts were not engaged. In fact, their primary motivation would appear to have been simply to maintain the institution that had been so carefully built up over the centuries by the religious hierarchy, and to safeguard Israel's status as an independent political entity, until such time as God should restore it as an autonomous world power—which was what they wanted him to do. Whatever language they employed, their thinking was basically secular. They are a classic example of the religious but faithless. It is a spirit that is still strongly in evidence today.

To give an example of what I mean by this, I was told recently of a couple whose relationship had broken down after thirty years of marriage. Now the husband is a very shy, reticent man who does not find it easy to share his feelings with others. Needless to say, in this situation, he found it virtually impossible to talk to anyone at all because he was so deeply hurt by what had taken place. However, it was a fact that he had tried extremely hard to keep the marriage going, and in the end it had been the wife who left. The wife, however, immediately began to tell everyone how it had all been his fault. She omitted to mention that she had left him. The result was that she succeeded in completely turning against him the church to which they both belonged. Their response was to ostracise him, and to demand that he repent. The extraordinary thing is that no one at any point sat down and talked *with* him, but rather he found himself judged and abandoned by those he had felt to be his friends. The fellowship as a whole, in fact, applied a blanket theology to the situation as they perceived it. Divorce was wrong. He was to blame. Therefore the sinner should be excluded from the fellowship. Event over. But it was not so clear cut as that, and both partners actually needed help and support at this point, if they were to come to a right place with God. The result has been a very deeply wounded man, who was blamed for something that was not exclusively his fault—as the wife had made it appear.

To return, however, to the main point, the way we see Satan working through and exploiting this basic self-centredness is masterly. Time and again we see people, motivated by what they see as a justifiable desire to maintain their own position and status, becoming a ready tool in the devil's hands. It is not a case of all these people being possessed. They still have free will, and that is an important point to make. But their predisposition towards self, which springs from evil, makes them all too ready to co-operate with suggestions the devil implants in their minds.

For example, the devil so built up the Pharisees' fear and hatred of Jesus, justifying it on the grounds that his teachings would stir up the people and thus endanger national security, that he brought them as a body to the point of manufacturing false accusations against him (Matthew 26:59–61). But the position is rather more complex than outright and deliberate rejection of what God was saying, because it would appear that their hardness of heart actually made them incapable of recognising that God was at work. For example, the Pharisees accused Jesus of casting out demons by Beelzebub (Matthew 13:24f.). Now the interesting thing is that there is no hint of deception here (apart from the deception operative upon their own minds). They surely believed what they were saying! This is interesting, because it is frequently the response of the religious spirit when God is powerfully at work. So where is this coming from?

At one level it is easy to say that the Pharisees were again being used by Satan. Jesus himself classed their words as the 'unforgivable sin against the Holy Spirit', so this is obviously true. But we cannot lay *all* the blame at Satan's door. The initial problem arose from the independent response of sinful nature, which made these men 'vulnerable' to the suggestions implanted by Satan. But there was something more at work here, and to get a clearer picture we need to look forward to Romans 1:18ff., where Paul gives a powerful insight into the workings and effect of sin on the human mind.

In this passage, Paul states that because of men and women's innate sinfulness, leading to the rebellious exercise of wrong choice, *God has darkened these individuals' understanding.* That is, he has withdrawn the protection and guidance of the Spirit so that, when the devil tempts them again, they are no longer capable of perceiving that their feet are firmly set on the road to hell. In fact, they think that what is evil is good! This is without doubt extremely serious, and we see this a lot today. For example, I was recently reading a report on pornography which contained interviews with five different men. Each one reported that as he had given way to the attractions of this literature, he had found himself being led into progressively more deviant forms of sexual behaviour. Two had even come to the point where they could no longer experience sexual arousal without the accompaniment of some sort of sexual perversion.

The point is that men and women's own rebelliousness makes them highly suggestible when the devil is at work, but, at least initially, they retain free will and may choose whether or not to respond. However, Satan's hold intensifies as they do respond and, if they persist in that response, they will inevitably come to a point where they cannot break free unaided.

To return, however, to the false accusations lodged against Jesus, it should also be noted that in this context, the devil did not operate through wildly untrue and outlandish suggestions that had no foundation in fact, but through a subtle twisting and perversion of things that had been both said and done, and which were therefore highly difficult to refute, precisely because at their heart there was a kernel of truth. For example, one of the charges brought against Jesus in support of the accusation of heresy at his trial was that he said, 'I am able to destroy the temple of God and rebuild it in three days' (Matthew 26:61). Now from John 2:19–21 we know that Jesus was actually speaking of the temple of his body, but that is not immediately apparent from the way his words were presented by his accusers. If, however, someone simply asked him, 'Did you say this?' what could he say? Of course he did!

This kind of twisting of the truth is unquestionably demonic in origin—not for nothing is Satan called 'the father of lies'. In the course of ministry I have not infrequently come across troubled individuals who regularly go around a whole host of different people reporting what has apparently been said and done. In the process they twist the true facts beyond all recognition, so that the result is absolute chaos, with everyone accusing everyone else of all sorts of extraordinary things. These troubled individuals are not to be blamed. I believe they cannot help themselves. But such situations require careful handling if they are not to result in enormous damage. The only way we can actually deal with this kind of situation is with total honesty, making it clear that we will not be party to any kind of 'secret' confidences, no matter how flattering these communications might be.

4. Confrontation

The final part of the devil's strategy was confrontation. We see this supremely in the cross, and all the gospels have a sense of gathering gloom as Jesus begins his last journey towards Jerusalem. But time and again before the final encounter at the cross we see preliminary skirmishes breaking out. For example, as Jesus crosses with the disciples to the country of the Gerasenes, he is met by a demon-possessed man who runs out to meet him from the tombs. We are told that this particular man is very strong. Prior to this meeting, the narrative says, he has been kept chained hand and foot in an effort to restrain him, but each time he has broken free. Elsewhere, Jesus himself makes a comparison between Satan and the 'strong man' who has wrongly taken possession of the house (Luke 11:21–22). Therefore, what is implied in this poor man is a physical embodiment of that same demonic power—the strong man who has wrongly taken possession of the house. The strong man (in the person of the demoniac) comes *out* to Jesus and challenges him, 'What do you want with me, Jesus, Son of the Most High God?' (Luke 8:28). It is an echo of the derisory challenge of the fallen but powerful angel to the incarnate Word of God, delivered through an individual whose will and body have both been totally overwhelmed.

We can almost feel Jesus' outrage at what has been done to this man, and his compassion for him. Again, as with Peter, he does not address the man, but instead speaks to the controlling demonic force behind. However, this is a very different situation to what was happening with Peter, and Jesus recognises this. The strong man has taken control of the house, yet it is not Satan himself who is present, but lesser spirits who serve him. Consequently, Jesus does not directly address Satan (which would be inappropriate), but instead tells the demonic spirit infesting and controlling the man to identify itself (for a fuller discussion of demons and their relationship to Satan, see Chapter 11). We learn that there are several demons present, who identify themselves by the name of Legion, begging Jesus not to send them to the abyss—the place of confinement for those in rebellion against God. Now this may be Satan's kingdom, but these are foot soldiers we have here, not the commander-in-chief, and Jesus responds appropriately by allowing them to go and infest a large herd of pigs, with the result that they all rush down the side of a hill headlong into the lake and are drowned. That is, he returns them to their proper element, but does not at this time consign them to the abyss and destruction. (The spirits themselves of course are not drowned, but merely the pigs which they are infesting. Deprived of human habitation the demonic spirits are then returned to their proper sphere of existence—of which water, to the ancient mind, was a symbol. Again, for a fuller discussion on this point see Chapters 9 and 11 below.)

We shall return to this incident later, in discussing both hell and the nature of demons. Here the point to be made is that for once the demons are not forced into the open by Jesus' presence, but actually come out to meet and challenge him. They must have reckoned that Satan's hold was pretty well complete; but actually faced by Jesus himself it was no contest, because they immediately capitulated before his power. If the demons recognised Jesus before that final confrontation on the cross, how much more are they forced to do so today, now that the victory has been decisively won?

Prior to the cross, however, such open and blatant confrontation is rare. More usually we see evidence of Satan and his minions' hold through the presence of sickness and death, the working of deception, and the wrongful exercise of power. Yet the final contest was inevitable from the moment of Jesus' birth, and Jesus himself clearly knew this. To use again the passage referred to above, in Luke 11:21–22, Jesus says clearly: 'When a strong man, fully armed, guards his own house, his possessions are safe. But when someone stronger attacks and overpowers him, he takes away the armour in which the man trusted and divides up the spoils.'

Jesus, then, explicitly identified the strong man with Satan—but he knew that he himself was 'the stronger', who drove out the demonic hordes by the finger of God. Yet it must be true that before the final confrontation on the cross, Satan did not fully appreciate this fact and so, in the gathering gloom of the last months, we see the prince of this world, apparently certain of victory, marshalling all his demonic forces for the final onslaught.

Crucifixion

It is all very well for us to try to rationalise the cross today and to see in Jesus' death the perfect example of obedience and forgiveness. But if we stop there his death reduces either to an incalculable cruelty on the part of God, or to some transcendent and painless charade that divests Jesus of his humanity and robs the whole act of meaning. All the evidence, in fact, suggests that Jesus saw his death in very different terms. He saw it as a terrible conflict that he might actually lose (see, for example, Luke 22:41–44, where we are told that as Jesus was praying, he was in such distress that his sweat was like drops of blood). Jesus would have had reason to fear, because he knew exactly who it was he was going to face, and he knew too that he was going to have to carry the full weight of our sin, and that it would involve his being separated from God. But he would appear also to have known that this was the only way that Satan's hold could be broken. Up to this point, he had had several encounters with Satan's followers, but he had not before come face to face with their lord himself. Yet that was why he had come (John 14:30). So for Jesus the cross was his final meeting with the strong man himself, and the triumph of life over death. This was the understanding of the apostles as they wrestled with the fact of Christ's death and their own anointing with the Holy Spirit. As summed up by the writer of Revelation, Jesus 'freed us from our sins by his blood' (Revelation 1:5).

On the cross Satan was defeated, and although that is by no means the entire significance of the cross, it does mean that today we can rely with total assurance on that victory. Until the time of final judgement there will inevitably be encounters with the strong man for all of us in our Christian lives, but we should never forget nor be diverted from the fact that the victory has already been attained.

7
Satan Exposed

One way in which we may better understand who the devil is, is in and through the names ascribed to him. In the New Testament we see a wide variety of names used, highlighting different attributes, and revealing much about the devil's character, activities, and the way in which he was generally perceived.

The devil's attributes

The gospel writers and Jesus himself drew freely on these names. After Jesus had been baptised, for example, he was driven by the Holy Spirit into the wilderness to be tempted by the *devil* (Matthew 4:1; Luke 4:1; Mark 1:13). This of course fits in perfectly with the role of the satan that we have already come across in the Old Testament. It was God himself who led Jesus into this time of testing, in order that he might be more fully prepared for the work that lay ahead—but it was the satan who carried it out. That is his work. Yet although this period was necessary and ordained by God, the presence of Satan and his enthusiasm for his work were clearly malevolent. Conspicuously, Jesus did not welcome him with open arms, and from the beginning of the trials there was hostility and an element of contest.

In Mark we read that Jesus was in the desert being tempted by Satan, but the other gospels specifically refer to the devil, although in Matthew, when Jesus finally addressed the devil directly and told him to be gone, he did say, 'Away from me, Satan!' (Matthew 4:10). This is of particular note because prior to this, in the Old Testament, such a complete identification of the one with the other had not been made. In the Old Testament we have had references to 'the serpent', 'the ancient enemy of man' and 'the dragon'—and in Eden we have seen the tempter appear as a snake—but the satan (the angel accuser) has not been explicitly identified with the chaos monster. This of course fits with the lack of interest in evil as an independent force that is characteristic of the Old Testament, but it is still noteworthy, given the view that emerges so clearly in the gospels, that the satan and the serpent are not, prior to this, seen as the same. Now, however, right at the beginning of the New Testament, when the scene is set for the final great contest, that identification is made. We know, therefore, from this point on that the devil, the ancient enemy of men and women, *is* the tempter. This may seem obvious, put like this, but it is a point that is frequently ignored or overlooked—and yet it is of fundamental importance for any understanding we might have of the devil's character, because even now, when he springs out with what seems to be unprecedented power, it locates him firmly under the sovereignty of God.

Another common ascription of the time for the devil was *Beelzebub*. The ancient world, both Jewish and non-Jewish, was more than familiar with the idea of demons. These were spiritual entities, not always thought to be specifically malign (although some were undeniably seen as agents of evil), but existing in separation from and hostility to God. Moreover, pagan deities such as Astarte and Ishtar, in whose worship Israel from time to time became embroiled, were identified in later Jewish thought, not so much as other gods but as demons (eg, 1 Corinthians 10:19f.). In particular, by the first century AD the Jews had come to regard the heathen deity Beelzebub (whose precise origins remain obscure, but who, as 'lord of the flies', is most usually identified as a dung god of the Ekronites) as the prince of these demons. A charge frequently levelled against Jesus by his opponents was that he cast out demons by this same Beelzebub, the prince of demons. Thus:

> They brought him a demon-possessed man who was blind and mute, and Jesus healed him . . . when the Pharisees heard this, they said, 'It is only by Beelzebub, the prince of demons, that this fellow drives out demons.'
>
> Jesus knew their thoughts and said to them, 'Every kingdom divided against itself will be ruined, and every city or household divided against itself will not stand. If Satan drives out Satan, he is divided against himself. How then can his kingdom stand?' (Matthew 12:22–26; cf. Mark 3:23–27; Luke 11:17–22).

Again, we have now an explicit identification made between Beelzebub, the prince of demonic spirits hostile to God, and Satan, the angelic being whose role it is to test God's children. But we have also here, in Jesus' words, the acknowledgement of an 'organised kingdom' existing in opposition to God and presided over by Satan. So we now know that Satan is the dragon, or chaos monster. But, more than that, we know that he rules over a kingdom of demon spirits who exist in alienation from God, because Jesus has acknowledged this fact. Furthermore, this prince of demons would appear to be behind not just things such as magic and divination (which have always been expressly forbidden to the Jews), but also all pagan religion and superstitious practice. (We may deduce this because Satan was seen as one and the same with this mainstream and powerful pagan deity.) We also know that he exercises a terrible and malign hold over men and women, because it is he who has caused such terrible bondage, which can be shattered only by the delivering power of God: 'If I drive out demons by the Spirit of God, then the kingdom of God has come upon you' (Matthew 12:28).

However, this is by no means the end of the story, because we find a further insight into the devil's field of operations in John. In this gospel, Jesus describes himself as the 'light of the world' (8:12) but says that his kingdom is not of this world (18:36). By contrast, he calls Satan *the prince or ruler of this world* (12:31; 14:30; 16:11). We have already alluded to the Jewish tradition that saw Satan as having been appointed to some special task of oversight for the world (ie, placed in authority over the world by God himself), from which lofty position of pre-eminence he rebelled against God, attempting to usurp the Creator's position of sovereignty and arrogate power wrongfully to himself. Moreover, we know from this tradition that because of this sin, Lucifer/Satan was cast out of heaven and confined upon the earth for a brief period to await final judgement by God. Now, if it is this idea that is being alluded to by John, it would do much to explain the undeniably strong links that exist between the devil and this world. That is, the title conferred upon Satan by Jesus himself indicates an original legitimate appointment made by God.

If this is difficult to understand, we may perhaps draw an analogy from the Norman Conquest of England. Immediately after William of Normandy had captured the throne, he set about granting areas of land to various of his followers. Each appointment carried with it an appropriate title. They were then authorised to hold that land on the king's behalf. For all purposes they could use it as their own, but the land remained vested in the king and they were committed in allegiance to him. Should one of these nobles then have rebelled or acted improperly, it would not have invalidated the original appointment, unless and until the king himself were to remove him. The use of the title 'prince of this world' would then appear to acknowledge that original conferment of power, despite the fact that the exercise of that power has gone far beyond its initial grant. This analysis is of course speculative and derived from a combination of Jewish tradition and Scripture, but such an interpretation would do much to explain both the power Satan unquestionably wields, and his authority over the demon hordes that follow him.

In Ephesians 2:2 Satan is further described as 'the ruler of the kingdom of the air' and his spirit is said to be at work in those who are disobedient. First-century cosmology, and indeed for some centuries following, saw 'the air' as the area between heaven and earth. Satan had been cast out of heaven and no longer had access to God, but as a spiritual being far more powerful than mankind, his proper sphere remained the air, whence he had easy access to the earth. This title then indicates the spiritual dimension to his kingdom. It is a kingdom of darkness, and under his rule are the evil spirits in rebellion against God who inhabit this sphere. They are forbidden entry into heaven, but again, as spiritual beings, naturally occupy the space between heaven and earth.

Other names ascribed to Satan include 'the *evil one*' (eg, Matthew 13:19), '*deceiver*' (2 Corinthians 11:3), '*tempter*' (eg, Matthew 4:3) and '*murderer*' (eg, John 8:44). From all these titles we learn that Satan is the enemy of mankind, who wants only our destruction and death, and who will stop at nothing to achieve that end. Further, in relation to his attempts to achieve this, Paul warns us that Satan can all too easily masquerade as an '*angel of light*' (eg, 2 Corinthians 11:14). Satan, he indicates, is perfectly capable of appearing before us as an angel of God, or even of trying to mimic God's voice itself. This is one of the reasons why Scripture warns us over and over again to 'test the spirits'. What this means in practice is that if we feel we have some divine revelation or prophecy, it is both right and proper to maintain a healthy scepticism and to test it, both by holding up what we have received against Scripture, and by sharing it with others whose opinion we respect. God does not require us to throw common sense out of the window.

The 'angel of light' today

As we grow in knowledge of God, we shall find that we can discern when he is speaking to us, and when it is just our imagination, or something worse. But there can be some real upsets for people in coming to that point, and it has been known for entire fellowships to be deceived, and then to feel cruelly let down when something they feel God has apparently promised fails to materialise. I believe it is an unhealthy aspect of spiritual life today that we have become a people who seek after signs. In the course of ministry I not infrequently come across people who seem to be almost continually seeking guidance. Now I am not saying that we should not seek the Lord's direction for our lives, because of course we should, but the proper attitude actually is quiet obedience, as so powerfully demonstrated by Jesus himself. God does guide, and as we grow in holiness, so we become more conscious of the purposes he has for our lives. But that guidance has to be in God's timing, and by his choice. There may well be times when God apparently chooses to withhold specific guidance. This does not necessarily mean that there is some terrible sin hanging over us that we need to repent of in order for this situation to change. On the contrary, it might simply mean that God wishes us to walk for a while in darkness with our hand in his, incapable of seeing a step ahead, and therefore relying on him alone.

To know God is to be in a real and dynamic relationship with him, but to be continually expecting signs is actually simply a form of magic, which the devil is quick to build on. I have long subscribed to the teachings of medieval mystics who told their disciples in prayer resolutely to ignore all kinds of emotional experience or blinding flashes of revelation. The reason for this was simple, and was certainly not that they did not expect anything of this nature to happen. But Satan, they taught, can appear as an angel of light and divert us from the path God has laid before us with all sorts of apparently noble and inspired ideas. If these suggestions are from Satan, we shall be able to turn away and they will leave an unease deep in our spirit. But if it is God who is speaking, we will not be able to turn away because, wherever we look, he will be there, and there will be a quality of sweetness and quiet truth to the experience that will find an echo in our soul.

It does happen like this. And, while not in any way wishing to dampen charismatic ardour, if we could all learn first the necessity for obedience and to trust God's love—rather than looking all the time for divine revelation and only, almost as an afterthought, seeking after holiness of life—many hurtful and damaging mistakes would be avoided.

If we are unsure as to a particular course of action and God seems remarkably 'quiet', we simply carry on with the original task in hand, or remain in the original situation. If God wants us to change, he will very soon let us know. After all, he is God. Similarly, if we are praying for others and are unsure how to proceed, the one thing we must not do is put forward a vague idea floating around at the back of our minds in the language, 'God is saying to me . . . '

Not so long ago someone came to see me who had been thinking of getting married, and had been really unsure whether or not to go ahead. He had asked a friend to pray with him, and she had passed on to him what she said was a word from the Lord, encouraging him to ask the girl and promising a blissfully happy marriage within a matter of months. On the strength of this he had proposed, and then the whole relationship had collapsed, leaving him feeling devastated. His prayer partner later admitted that her encouragement had not actually come from any specific word in prayer, but simply from a general sense that they went so well together. The one thing we all need to ask for above everything else is discernment. It is a gift that God really does want to give.

What else does Satan do?

We have seen how Satan attacked Jesus, and the battle plan he adopted exposes only too well how he still operates today. Satan remains the great deceiver and will try in every way he can to fool us into believing that things are other than they are. Especially, he will attempt to disrupt and destroy relationships, using such weapons as doubt, jealousy, bitterness, resentment, lack of forgiveness, self-interest and the like. It is surely no accident that today we see so many families falling apart and so many individuals feeling that they cannot cope alone.

The devil remains the destroyer. He tries to destroy the love we feel for others, and our trust in them. He tries to destroy the love we feel for God, attempting to convince us that God himself has forsaken us and does not care. He tries to destroy the proper love we should feel for ourselves . . . and his ultimate goal is to fool us into destroying ourselves.

He remains, however, capable of holding before us all sorts of things that superficially appear good and that feed our sense of power and of being 'in control'. For example, he will give to us things that appear good—especially in the early days as he establishes and consolidates control. These things may include revealing the future to us through tarot, healing through manipulation of psychic energies, or an affluent lifestyle through the single-minded pursuit of status and money. Yet all these things serve ultimately only to bind us to death and it is indescribably sad that people should gain, as they think, the world, only to discover finally that they have given allegiance to the usurper prince who hates them and whose will is to destroy.

Jesus, by his life and teaching, threw a spotlight on the devil. It was not that the devil had changed in either status or activities from the time he first slithered into Eden, but the full extent of his hatred had been hidden. We learn, then, important things from the ways in which Jesus described Satan, and from the names ascribed to him in general throughout the New Testament—things that are relevant for us today. The devil would still like to fool us into believing either that he is not there, or that he is not such a bad chap after all. However, his essential character and implacable hostility are both revealed in his conflict with Jesus, and we must not lose sight of that today. It is only by that knowledge that we are armed to stand against Satan, and only by holding to that knowledge that we can use the power God wishes, through Jesus, to give to us. However, before moving on in our examination of Satan, let us summarise our understanding so far.

The story so far

Lucifer was created by God one of the most powerful angels. It would appear that he may have been appointed by God to a special position of oversight for the earth. He grew jealous of God's creative powers, and seems to have resented the creation of men and women as spiritual but incarnate beings. He challenged God, trying to rise to a position of pre-eminence, and drawing to himself in the process a group of similarly minded, but less powerful, rebellious angels. There was conflict in heaven, which resulted in Lucifer and his group being cast out of heaven by Michael and the heavenly host (see Revelation 12:7) and being hurled down to the earth.

Along with Lucifer, from this point on he acquired a number of names, all of which describe various aspects of his nature and activities (eg, adversary, accuser, etc). Although convicted of rebellion, he remains a part of the heavenly host and as such has to be obedient to God (that is, he cannot act beyond prescribed limits—see Job 6). His sphere of operations now would appear to be confined to the earth, where he attempts in every way to oppose God's rule and divert worship to himself, but his existence remains in the heavenly places. However, there is a time already fixed for future judgement, when God will cleanse, redeem and restore the whole of creation. That process was initiated by the coming of Christ, God's creative Word made flesh. On the cross, Jesus met with Satan face to face, and once and for all broke his power. Yet although the decisive battle has been fought and men and women can live in freedom as they turn to the crucified Lord, the world is still under occupation as God works now to reclaim his own before he executes final judgement and destroys Satan and all his works.

So, in the engagement of the devil with Christ, the nature of the conflict is exposed. There is still conflict today, and to many in the world it looks as if evil is winning. But Satan's days are numbered. He has already been defeated and we all need to realise this fact, not just with our heads, but in our hearts and emotions as well. God is sovereign, and the final destiny of Satan and his demonic hordes has already been determined. It is when we realise this that we come into freedom and into the power of God.

Many Christians feel tremendous fear about anything to do with Satan or demons, and we are absolutely right to have a healthy respect for these spiritual powers— they are not just figments of the imagination, and men and women do get both deceived and hurt. Jesus himself got hurt! But the battle is not ours, it is God's, and it has already been won. Satan knows that, along with all his followers, and he has to yield before the name of Christ. It is because of this that we do not ever need to feel frightened as we stand in Jesus' name and claim the victory with the assurance that comes from the certainty of his love.

8
The Devil and Hell

A few years ago some of the Monty Python comedy team made a film called *Time Bandits*. Towards the end Satan appeared, and as I recall, he had a rather natty head-dress and a splendid red cloak. He also had an overriding interest in computers and modern technology, and from his head office down in hell he was spearheading a campaign to take over the market and achieve world domination. While he gathered with the executive committee, his lesser minions were having a ball. In fact, it was definitely party time, with black leather and whips the order of the day! Hell was where the action was!

It's a funny thing: a lot of people today, if they think about it at all, actually visualise hell as a place of tremendous fun and debauchery (as if the two somehow went together); a sort of cosmic version of 'sex, drugs and rock 'n' roll'. Heaven, on the other hand, they regard as rather boring; full of vapid people sitting around on clouds and singing hymns all day. God is an old stick-in-the-mud, but the devil is a real raver. I have taken funerals where people have said jocularly, 'We're really going to miss old so-and-so. She was a really good person—tremendous sense of humour.

She'll be making the angels laugh now!' And then after a pause, 'Of course, I'll be going to the other place. All my friends'll be down there. I'm a bit too naughty for heaven!' Naturally, such people would then go on to disclaim any kind of religious faith at all, or excuse themselves by saying that they do not mean it. But it reflects some of the popular misconceptions about hell.

The traditional line, of course, is that hell is a place of torment and horror. Many people do still subscribe to this view, but, interestingly, almost everyone you talk to, on whichever side of the line they stand, regards Satan as the lord of this place—a domain to which he carries off the souls of all those he has managed to ensnare during their mortal lives.

If these views reflect popularist ideas, however, the point should equally be made that there are not a few Christians today who find the doctrine of hell acutely embarrassing, and refuse even to consider it because of this. The presence of a place of endless torment, they argue, is incompatible with the idea of an all-loving, all-powerful creator God. Therefore, either such a place does not exist at all, and if it did, it existed only up to the time of Christ's death, at which point the whole of mankind was redeemed, or else it is temporary—a place for the correction and refinement of the soul following on death, fitting the individual for entry into heaven. But of course Satan does not have any connection with it . . . because all too often, for these people, Satan does not exist. What we call evil is simply the absence of good.

Now all of these views have one thing in common: they have absolutely no foundation in the Bible at all. While it may be reassuring to convince ourselves that hell is either fun or does not exist, such ideas will fundamentally impair both the nature of our faith and our relationship with God. People tend to shy away from talking about hell because they find the idea of judgement both repugnant and frightening. But actually to understand biblical teaching on this whole area can only enrich our faith and establish us in real freedom. If we are engaged in any kind of spiritual warfare, we need to know both what hell is and the nature of Satan's relationship to this place. So let us have a look at what the Bible says.

Hell in the Old Testament

We are so used to thinking in terms of resurrection and afterlife, that it often comes as a surprise to learn that the Old Testament does not have any clearly developed doctrine of the hereafter. Rather, the underlying idea would appear to be that if men and women were created as spiritual beings in God's image, then in fellowship with him they could and would share in his eternity.

Taken by itself, the flesh was nothing. The individual was given independent animation by the breath of life, which came from God himself: '. . . the Lord God formed the man from the dust of the ground and breathed into his nostrils the breath of life, and the man became a living being' (Genesis 2:7; cf. Ezekiel 37:7–10). It followed that what was perceived as death was simply the withdrawal of that breath, and its effects could equally well be felt when men and women were physically alive, as when their bodies had in every sense returned to dust. An oft-repeated cry of the psalmist for example is, 'You cast me down to Sheol (see below) .' But equally he asserts his belief that God can restore him from there to life (eg, Psalm 103:2-3). Beyond individual consciousness, meaning and identity were given to life by virtue of participation in the covenant community, by membership of one of the twelve tribes with whom God had made a unique and everlasting agreement that he would be their God, and would protect them while they remained faithful to him. In a very real sense to the Israelites, provided a man maintained his standing with God, he would not die because he would live on through his son, and the generations together made up a kind of eternal psychic entity. The underlying idea then for the individual was not so much of afterlife, but rather of the immortality of the soul, which was entirely dependent for its existence on the covenant and its relationship with God.

However, that bodies did not endure physically was inescapable, and the obvious question that began to nag at people's minds as they discovered they wanted a bit of individual reassurance was: What happened to people once they had died? The answer was Sheol, which in Israelite thought was the earliest designation for the realm to which the dead belonged.

Sheol

Sheol was the state and abode of death, and it was located in the underworld—you went *down* to Sheol. Throughout the ancient Near East we find similar ideas. The dead are pictured as existing in a dark, subterranean and rather frightening realm, ruled over by a dark and frightening, independent god. In Canaanite myth, for example, this realm is ruled over by Mot, the god of summer drought and destruction. But in the strongly monotheistic Jewish formulation, Sheol is ruled over by Yahweh. Now this is important to us because it establishes at the outset that although death (in the sense of separation from God) came into the world because of sin, at no point was the fallen angel, Lucifer, seen as holding independent power over a realm in isolation from God.

The Old Testament tells us poetically that Sheol is seen as located beneath the surface of the earth (eg, Psalm 86:13). It is dark (Job 10:21), a place of destruction (Psalm 18:4), utterly silent and gloomy (Psalm 94:17), and there the soul is lost in oblivion (Psalm 88:12). However, this state does not make all communication impossible with those who are still living, as demonstrated by Saul's calling up of Samuel through the witch of Endor. But while communication with souls in Sheol is possible, it is categorically forbidden: 'Let no-one be found among you who sacrifices his son or daughter in the fire, who practises divination or sorcery, interprets omens, engages in witchcraft, or casts spells, or who is a medium or spiritist or who consults the dead. Anyone who does these things is detestable to the Lord . . . ' (Deuteronomy 18:10–12).

Spiritists and mediums who engage in this activity, therefore, are clearly seen as under the influence of something other than God (eg, Acts 16:16). The penalty for such activity in early Israel was death (Deuteronomy 18:20) and later, as we know from the incident in Acts referred to above, the capacity for such communication was clearly perceived as a demonic hold from which people needed to be delivered or set free.

More specifically, Sheol was also sometimes seen as a place of punishment, in that those who were consigned to it prematurely were seen as under judgement (eg, Psalm 49:13–14). But it should be noted that the satan was not seen as having any influence or field of operation there—for the simple reason that it was within the world that the individual had the opportunity of responding to God, and the presence of the satan in Sheol would have been superfluous. Yahweh, however, is very much present in Sheol, and is able to deliver even from the hand of death: 'If I go up to the heavens, you are there; if I make my bed in the depths (Sheol), you are there' (Psalm 139:8; cf. Psalm 16:10).

The pit or abyss

In later Jewish literature we see a developing idea of separation within Sheol between the wicked and the righteous. In Ezekiel 32:14, for example, we find reference to 'the pit' as being a place of punishment. Such an idea, however, was not fully developed until comparatively late. Detailed descriptions of the abyss, for example, are first found in the inter-testamental book *Enoch*. Such ideas are, however, clearly widely accepted by this time and in turn are foundational to New Testament understanding of judgement, as expressed by both Jesus and later New Testament writers.

But from where do we get the association of the abyss with evil, and is this right? For an answer we need perhaps to look first at the religious ideas of some of the cultures surrounding Israel at this time, because they were clearly influential.

In Babylonian myth we see creation as coming about through a struggle between Marduk, the god of creation, and Tiamat, the dragon of chaos. Tiamat is overcome and takes up residence in the sea, the waters beneath the firmament. The peoples of the ancient world tended to dislike the sea. It was dangerous, and confined as they were in a frail boat when they ventured out on it, disaster could and frequently did overtake them. The Israelites, as we have already seen, shared this perception. For them the sea was the home of the dragon or chaos monster, a force hostile to God. This traditional belief persisted, and in the inter-testamental *Ascension of Moses* 10:6, for example, it says that in the end time, when the forces hostile to God are subdued, the sea will return to the abyss. This is important to our understanding, because it reflects the earliest understanding of the abyss as the place where the primeval waters that surrounded the earth were confined by God as a part of the process of creation (see Genesis 1:6–7). They then formed a kind of subterranean sea separated off from the dry land by a firmament. The point of interest, however, is that developing Jewish thought saw the forces in rebellion against God as inhabiting this element (eg, Psalm 74:13–14).

By the time of Isaiah (24:21–22), the abyss has become a dungeon where the rebellious powers of heaven *and* the kings of the earth are bound and herded together as punishment for their disobedience to God. It has become a special place of punishment, ruled over by God. A far more vivid description, however, is provided by the inter-testamental writer Enoch. The abyss or pit, as he describes it, is the special place of confinement for fallen angels, namely, those who have sinned by having seduced mortal women and thereby bringing about the birth of the nephilim (the terrible and terrifying race of giants who, according to legend, walked the earth prior to the Flood, being identified with the people reported in Genesis 6:4), and those who have taught men and women to worship demons. It is a place entirely devoid of creation, the end of heaven and earth—waste and desolate. In every sense it is the embodiment of chaos, with no firmament above and no earth beneath (Enoch 18:12–16). As described by Enoch, it has become a kind of spiritual black hole, into which all the angels and powers that have rebelled are bound hand and foot and thrown (Enoch 88:1). Again, there is no suggestion at this point of the lordship of Satan over this place. The abyss is rather an intermediate place of punishment for rebellious elements. Final judgement lies ahead. This, however, is rather to anticipate the line of reasoning and, before attempting to draw any conclusions, we need to examine the ideas underlying *Hinnom* and *Hades*.

Hinnom

Hinnom is a Hebrew word, translated in the New Testament as Gehenna. Its exact meaning is obscure, although originally it was probably the name of an individual. Subsequently, it became the designation for a valley south of Jerusalem which for centuries functioned as a place for pagan child sacrifice by fire to the god Moloch. In Jewish thought it was a place of horror and abomination, but that did not stop them, at various periods in their history, from becoming embroiled in the practice themselves. In 2 Kings 16:3–4, for example, we read that Ahaz burned his own son, hoping in this way to assuage the divine wrath that had apparently come upon the nation: 'He walked in the ways of the kings of Israel and even sacrificed his son in the fire, following the detestable ways of the nations the Lord had driven out before the Israelites. He offered sacrifices and burned incense at the high places, on the hilltops and under every spreading tree.'

Prior to this (2 Kings 3:26–27) we have come across a

Moabite king doing exactly the same thing in a vain attempt to secure victory against Israel. And later we know from Jeremiah 7:18–31 that Jehoiakim, the evil king of Israel, also followed the blasphemous religion of Moloch: 'They have built the high places of Topheth in the Valley of Ben Hinnom to burn their sons and daughters in the fire—something I did not command, nor did it enter my mind' (Jeremiah 7:31).

The Israelites only began fully to appreciate how evil this practice was in the reign of Josiah. This king, in an attempt to purify Yahwistic religion, ended all forms of pagan sacrifice in the valley of Hinnom and defiled the whole area. Following on from that time, it became used as a vast refuse pit and a place where the corpses of criminals and animals were burned. Hardly surprisingly, then, over time the name Hinnom began to be used among the Jews as a synonym for hell, and there was even a tradition current that the valley contained within it the mouth to hell itself. It was then but a short step for inter-testamental Jewish writers to use Hinnom, or Gehenna, as the name for the place within Sheol where sinners received their eternal punishment (eg, 2 Esdras 7:36), the unquenchable fires of judgement being an all-too-visible symbol before them in the fires that burned in the valley. Hell or Hades is the New Testament rendering of Gehenna, and its existence as a place of eternal and horrific punishment was accepted without question by both Jesus and his disciples (eg, Matthew 5:22; 10:28; Mark 9:43 ff.; Luke 12:5).

For Jesus, then, judgement was an integral and even foundational part of his worldview. It was not just a vague possibility, it was certain, and it was God's response to sin. God alone had the power to consign to hell, and he alone was to be feared because of this.

Hell, as taught by Jesus, is a place of torment and unquenchable fire (Mark 9:43–44). It is separated from heaven by an unbridgeable chasm, and there is no suggestion that those consigned to it will ever come out again. Thus, in the parable of the rich man and Lazarus, Abraham admonishes the pain-wracked Dives: ' . . . Son, remember that in your lifetime you received your good things, while Lazarus received bad things, but now he is comforted here and you are in agony. And besides all this, between us and you a great chasm has been fixed, so that those who want to go from here to you cannot, nor can anyone cross over from there to us' (Luke 16:25–26).

Hinnom or Gehenna would thus by extension appear to be the abyss or pit. It is a place of general and terrible punishment but, most importantly for our purposes here, it is the place of punishment for the devil and his demonic hordes. The demons, from the New Testament, would appear to know all about the abyss/hell, and it is the last place they want to go. For example, we have already seen how when Jesus heals the demon-possessed man in the region of the Gerasenes, the demons beg the Lord not to send them to the abyss. They are terrified, and Jesus responds by sending them into the pigs, who promptly all rush down to the water and drown, thus returning the demons for the time being to their proper element (Luke 8:26–33; see also Chapter 6 above. In order to avoid any confusion here, it should be underlined that there is a certain ambiguity in Jewish thought on this point. On the one hand they believed that the sea was inhabited by the forces hostile to God but, at the same time, from a cosmological perspective, they believed that the air—the technical term for the area between heaven and earth—was the proper sphere for those incorporeal spirits forbidden entry into heaven because of their rebellion against God).

Now we need at this point to return more specifically to our understanding of the pit, because this is by no means, for our purposes, the complete picture. We left the pit as a kind of spiritual black hole, a place of intermediate punishment. Intermediate, because we know from the New Testament writings that a time for final judgement has already been fixed, when God, as a part of his redemptive process, will remake the heavens and the earth, in the process destroying all that has been flawed. The clearest expression of this doctrine is found in Revelation, although prior to this Jesus himself has already referred to the coming cosmic showdown, when everything that is not of God will be destroyed. The time for this, he says, is known to the Father alone (eg, Mark 13; Luke 21:5-36; Matthew 24:1-51).

The teaching of Revelation is complex, but on one point at least it is very clear, and that is the final destiny of Satan and his followers. In Revelation many of our ideas about hell fall into place. For example, one idea that we find current in ancient Jewish thought (not in the Bible) was that stars were divine beings. In Revelation 9, the fifth angel who stands before God sounds his trumpet, and the star that had fallen from the sky to the earth is given the key to the shaft of the abyss (Revelation 9:1). We already know that in rabbinic tradition Lucifer was cast out of heaven for his rebellion and down to the earth, and that his fall was like that of a star (Isaiah 14:12-15). We can then infer that it is Satan who is being referred to here, and that for this time he is being given authority by God over the abyss—the place of punishment—itself. We should note that Satan himself is not in the abyss, but powers of evil most certainly are, and it is these that, by God's permission, he unleashes upon the earth in the form of demonic locusts. We have said before, of course, that those consigned to the abyss do not appear to be able to come out. This, however, is the one exception: where God himself orders their release. Yet even at this point these evil powers are under the authority of God, because they are forbidden to harm any plant-life, but may torture only those people who do not have the seal of God on their foreheads. In effect they are given permission to harm only those who presumably have given worship to Satan himself—and the aim on God's part is most clearly repentance. The locusts, however, are not well intentioned, and their leader is the angel of the abyss—Abaddon or Apollyon.

These two names come from the Hebrew word for destruction, and it is an interesting question whether the fallen star and Abaddon are one and the same or not. We shall presume they are, on the grounds that it was Lucifer who first initiated rebellion in heaven and drew after him other rebellious angels, and that the latter subsequently gave him their allegiance. On this line of reasoning, however, the demonic spirits, up to this point imprisoned in the abyss, have been separated from their lord by the fact of their incarceration. If this is right, there are clear implications for our ministry today. It is true that it is nowhere specifically recorded in the gospels that Jesus himself sent demonic spirits to the abyss, but equally clearly from this passage there are demonic spirits confined there, and from the gospels we know that the one thing such spirits feared above all else was to be sent there. We therefore conclude that not only can such spirits be cast out today, but they can also be bound in the authority of Christ and sent to this place of punishment where, for a time, they will be separated from their lord, Satan.

Following the narrative in Revelation, the sixth angel then unleashes the four angels who have been bound at the River Euphrates. In Jewish thought the Euphrates was the ideal boundary between Israel and bordering hostile powers. These angels then have been confined in an alien and distant place—but not the abyss. To backtrack a little, in the book of Enoch we find frequent reference to 'angels of punishment', whose job it is to unleash the avenging wrath of God upon the people. These four angels would appear to fall into this category. But are we to infer that they owe primary allegiance to Satan or to God? Again, the goal is repentance, but on balance it would seem that we can conclude they are a part of the elements that are in rebellion against God, because (like Satan) they are confined on the earth and do not have any part of heaven. However, prior to their unleashing, on God's authority, their destructive power has not been felt by mankind.

Both the timescale and time-patterning of Revelation are notoriously difficult, but the idea would appear to be that after a time of great tribulation upon the earth, during which time the forces of good and evil battle it out and Satan gains ascendancy over the hearts and minds of many, there will be a terrible confrontation between the armies of God and those who have deludedly given allegiance to the beast and the false prophet (we shall return to these in a minute). The result of this is that the two servants of the devil (that is, the beast and false prophet) responsible for all this wickedness are thrown into 'the fiery lake of burning sulphur'

(Revelation 19:20). This, however, is not yet the fate of Satan. Rather, he is seized by the angel who now holds the key to the abyss (at what point it has been taken from Satan we do not know), bound hand and foot, and thrown into the demonic prison house for the period of a thousand years. Why final judgement on Satan is deferred in this way is not clear, but following on his imprisonment the 'first resurrection' takes place. That is, all those who have died for their faith, or who have not worshipped the beast or his image nor received his mark, arise and reign in glory alongside Christ.

At the end of the thousand-year period, however, Satan is once again released from his prison and is allowed to go out and deceive the nations and gather them for the final battle (Revelation 20:7f.). Again they are overcome—this time by fire from heaven—and, like his minions before, Satan is now also cast into the lake of burning sulphur. We read that there 'they will be tormented day and night for ever and ever' (Revelation 20:10).

Only after all of this has happened does the final judgement of mankind take place. *All* those who have died now rise and stand before God. Death and Hades are emptied, and those who have now come to life are judged by what they have done in life (Revelation 20:13). The idea then is that the first phase of God's eternal judgement rests entirely on what men and women have done in life—in this sense, we write our own judgement. Then, death and Hades are thrown after Satan into the lake of fire (Revelation 20:14). That is, death and Hades (the abyss) are themselves destroyed. Now clearly, if we think back to the parable of the rich man and Lazarus told by Jesus (Luke 16:19–31), this is important because the rich man speaks from hell, where he is already receiving a foretaste of final judgement. We have already seen that it is impossible to pass from 'Abraham's side' to hell, but the implication from Revelation would appear to be that for both this was an intermediate state. The righteous have already experienced resurrection (Revelation 20:4ff.), but now this is the general resurrection, and specifically it concerns those who have been lost at sea (who according to ancient thought, as they had not received burial, were condemned to wander *between* earth and heaven in a kind of limbo) and those held by death and Hades.

However, before we rejoice and say, 'So everybody does get resurrected after all!' we should read on. Hades has been destroyed, but now the judgement continues. The second book is opened, the Book of Life. All those whose names are not found written in this book are now also thrown into the lake of fire.

So it is not hell that is the final place of punishment, but the lake of fire. That is reserved for Satan and his demonic hordes, and for all those who have not only committed wrongful acts, but who have also during the period of their lives upon earth *not made any kind of commitment to the true God*. The idea underlying the Book of Life comes from the common practice of rulers in the ancient world of keeping a roll-book of living citizens under their control. When a man or woman died, their name would be removed. So here, the idea is of a record of those who have given allegiance to God, and all those whose names are not found there are quite simply given over to destruction.

I believe we need to take this very seriously indeed. First, the symbol used highlights the importance of making a real commitment to God in the person of Jesus Christ during the period of our lives upon earth.

Second, it suggests that we need also to maintain that commitment. Such roll-books were, by definition, a living record. The analogy therefore suggests that even having once made that commitment, if we subsequently deliberately turn away and deny Christ, it is entirely possible (though not certain) that our names will be removed from the record of those destined for eternal salvation (cf. Galatians 5:21). Commitment does not mean perfection, but it does mean an active and continuing faith—and a genuine attempt at obedience to Christ.

The fact that God has given us the gift of free will must mean that he will respect our choice to be ultimately separate from him.

Resurrection

The one point that may cause some puzzlement is how we have arrived at any doctrine of resurrection, given that we have said there is no developed doctrine of the hereafter in the Old Testament. The answer is simple, and has to do with the inescapable fact of suffering and the Jewish perception of evil. Over the years it became apparent to everyone that the righteous, despite what the rabbis said, all too frequently did not receive their just reward during the period of this life. However, the unrighteous—not to mention positively evil—all too frequently did prosper, both in material goods and in plain old-fashioned fun. Something clearly was not working, and the book of Job especially is an attempt to understand and deal with the whole question of undeserved suffering. It will be remembered that Job prospered at the end of his life—but many did not, and indeed over the centuries the nation itself was crippled by foreign aggression, despite the people's best efforts (as they saw it) to be faithful to the covenant religion. Both individual and national hope therefore became shifted into the future. The rabbis began to teach that whatever unfairnesses there might be in this life, God was faithful, and just reward and punishment would become apparent in the hereafter. More than that, the fortunes of Israel would be miraculously restored under the leadership of a messiah—a second David anointed by God to restore the kingdom to God's chosen people.

Initially, then, the idea of resurrection evolved as an eschatological (end-time) hope tied to the rebirth of the nation, but it extended to encompass individual life. By the time of Jesus, the Pharisees at least were teaching a doctrine of resurrection, although this was not accepted by the Sadducees (eg, Matthew 22:23-33; Mark 12:18-27; Luke 20:27-38). More to the point, Jesus himself not only endorsed this doctrine, but gave form to it in and through his own life. By his crucifixion, he ushered in the resurrection, thereby demonstrating that he had shattered for evermore the hold of death brought in by sin. He broke open the gates of hell, not because they had been closed up by Satan, but because the operation and presence of sin made separation and judgement inevitable. God's wrath was triggered by sin. His nature was such that he could not compromise with it, and that which was sinful could not co-exist in his presence. Before Christ by his death bore the penalty of that sin and restored men and women who took up his offer to a state of righteousness, the only destiny for sinful man was Hades.

In conclusion, therefore, Satan is not the lord of Sheol, or the pit—but he is lord of the dark and evil powers confined there, because it is to him that they have given their allegiance. But his rebellious and destructive authority extends only to the limits of the earth. According to Scripture, it is not Satan who torments those who are in hell, but the suffering experienced is a consequence of sin against God and the resulting separation from God. That there is a punitive element in this is inescapable. It is the judgement of God on rebellion. The judgement is reserved primarily for Satan and his fallen angelic host. God has an absolute will to save men and women from that judgement and redeem us from Satan's hold. We are, however, at perfect liberty to reject that—and God will respect our decision. We can, therefore, write our own judgement during the period of this life by rejecting God's overtures and discipline and following instead the false goods of Satan, who does all in his power to hijack the worship we should properly be giving to God. Until final judgement is passed upon Satan and all those who have given him allegiance, the pit (or Hades) would appear to be a kind of cosmic remand centre where offenders are detained pending their trial and passing of sentence. It is not a good place to be.

Antichrist

Is Satan the Antichrist? In 2 Thessalonians, Paul tackles the question of the timing of the Second Coming. Obviously the expectation of Christ's imminent return in glory was proving unsettling, but the apostle warns the Thessalonians:

> Don't let anyone deceive you in any way, for that day will not come until the rebellion occurs and the man of lawlessness is revealed, the man doomed to destruction. He

will oppose and will exalt himself over everything that is called God or is worshipped, so that he sets himself up in God's temple, proclaiming himself to be God ... The coming of the lawless one will be in accordance with the work of Satan displayed in all kinds of counterfeit miracles, signs and wonders, and in every sort of evil that deceives those who are perishing (2 Thessalonians 2:3–4, 9–10).

The Antichrist idea is given clearest expression in Revelation, from chapter 10 onwards, but it is interesting that both Paul and John foretell the coming of a 'man of sin', who will exalt himself and claim the worship that belongs to God, deceiving men and women by counterfeit signs and miracles. This figure is the embodiment of evil.

In the letters of John, however, we have reference not just to one, but to many antichrists, who can be recognised by the fact that they deny that Jesus is the Christ (eg, 1 John 2:18–23). This would appear to be an extension of the same sort of idea found in first-century Judaism of there being many messiahs; that is, individuals powerfully anointed by God for a specific task of salvation. Jesus, however, so far transcended common expectations as to give a wholly different meaning to the word. As applied to Jesus, the term 'Messiah' meant 'unique and incarnate Son of God'. The term 'antichrist', then, as used by the apostles, would appear to indicate certain individuals *anointed* by Satan for a specific work of drawing away the faithful.

In Revelation we find a significant deepening of this concept. As Jesus is the incarnation of the word of God, so now we may assume that this individual becomes, through powerful anointing, the physical embodiment of Satan. In Revelation 11:7 the Antichrist/beast comes up from out of the abyss and has terrible destructive power; he kills the two prophets. But, more specifically, in Revelation 13 we have the image of the beast coming up from out of the sea (the home of the chaos monster) and being given *authority* by the dragon (13:4–8). He makes war upon the saints (the church) and because of him men worship the dragon, whose authority he wields.

The image, then, as has already been said, is of an individual who, in his person, is the embodiment of evil. In him physically is manifested all the power opposed to God—but he is nevertheless to be distinguished from Satan. Satan remains an angelic and therefore incorporeal being, but the Antichrist is a visible figure upon earth, who must at some point willingly have given total allegiance to his dark lord (it should be remembered that Satan cannot create, and should not therefore be seen as having called this individual into existence). As the name suggests, he is the visible antithesis of the incarnate Christ: Satan's follower anointed for the purposes of evil. He differs from ordinary men and women in that spiritually he is the essence of evil. There is no suggestion of battle for his soul, nor even of the possibility of redemption, because he is united in being with Satan. He is not merely swayed by evil, he *is* evil, because of his total identification with his lord. With God's permission, he has been called up by Satan out of the abyss. It would appear that the decision for him was made long ago.

The overall idea would appear to be that over the centuries Satan uses many specially anointed tools for his evil purposes. These men and women, who have given their total allegiance to this dark lord, are 'antichrists', and they draw many away from God by their teachings and influence. But in the end times, it is foretold that the man of sin (or lawlessness), whom we may call *the Antichrist*, will be called up by Satan from out of the abyss. He will so far transcend his predecessors in evil and power as to give a whole new meaning to the term. He will be the physical embodiment (though not incarnation) of Satan himself, wielding his power. His coming will be a time of terrible test and will herald the final great battle—when Satan himself is to be bound and cast into the pit for a thousand years.

There are many antichrists today, though I believe we have yet to see the coming of 'the Antichrist'. They teach ideas that lead men and women away from the truth that is to be found only in God. Yet it is precisely because of this that these servants of evil are identifiable. As we have already seen, in the antichrists' opposition to God, no matter how seductive the ideas they peddle may appear, their clearest distinguishing mark is their absolute denial of the reality of the incarnation. We would do well to take this seriously. In this day and age we are seeing the spread of many attractive ideas and philosophies. Many people are being seduced into following all sorts of really quite bizarre practices on the promises of happiness, health and the achievement of ambition. It can indeed appear hard to fault some of these practices because they are presented in so sanitised a form and are so all-embracing of other spiritual teachings and beliefs. We have arrived at the 'whatever works for you' mentality, where there is a denial of absolute truth. But what is cloaked in tolerance is actually a total rejection of any other form of truth, and especially of the Christian conception of God.

Many people who have become caught up in the

various New Age teachings and ideas actually express tremendous admiration for Christ—but the one thing that is remarkable is that they all deny his uniqueness. There really does seem to be an unbridgeable divide here. People will happily acknowledge that Jesus was 'enlightened', but as a result of all the teachings they have imbibed they are prevented from seeing anything else—especially that his death achieved anything of unrepeatable significance. This means that despite their aspirations, they remain separated from God.

I am aware that this may seem a little harsh, but I really do believe that we are seeing in these teachings the seduction of Antichrist; and, although some of these appear extremely attractive, spiritually men and women stand in terrible danger. I believe we should identify these modern gurus with the antichrists specifically warned against in the Bible, and we can recognise them by their categorical denial to acknowledge the uniqueness of Christ.

An encounter with a man from the Findhorn Community in Scotland all too clearly demonstrated the problem. Findhorn is easily the biggest New Age teaching centre in the United Kingdom, and probably one of the biggest in the world. As well as running an almost continuous spiritual educational programme, its members regularly produce some very sizable vegetables, which they attribute to their communication and harmony with nature spirits. These spirits, they claim, regularly manifest themselves, and chief among these manifestations is the nature god, Pan.

As I was talking to this gentleman, he claimed that they were all serving God, so I asked him what he thought about Jesus. 'Fantastic!' he said. 'He was one of the Enlightened Ones.' In no way would he acknowledge that Jesus was unique; neither could he see any need for his redemptive death. Jesus was a son of God, he said, in the same way that we are all sons of God; the only difference between him and ourselves was that he had fully realised it. By this alone, and if for no other reason, irrespective of any communication with spirits, I believe we should recognise that such teachings are demonic in origin and in that sense come straight from hell.

Again, I am aware that this will upset some people, and not a few who claim to be Christian, but these teachings separate from God and open the individual up to demonic influence and hold. So many people who follow teachings of this nature do so from the highest of motives—they want the same peace and joy that we all want. The trouble is that though initially these teachings can seem to bestow all sorts of benefits, and give to the individual a sense of power, ultimately they are serving the fallen angel of destruction, who wants only to get a stranglehold on their lives and, through them, the whole of creation. To follow such teachings binds one to death.

9
Angels

In the 1940s the German theologian Rudolph Bultmann, in his attempts to 'demythologise' the gospels, announced that there was no place in the modern world for such things as angels and demons. For a long time 'modern man' believed him . . . but modern man also announced that God was dead, displaced by the power of intellect and science.

I believe that in this century Western culture and thought have been the focus of the most tremendous demonic attack, and by and large we have swallowed the lies hook, line and sinker. We have bought into the myth that science will give us total control over every area of our lives, whatever that might mean—perfect bodily health, optimum population control, fair distribution of resources . . . even global peace. Modern man rejected God, but unfortunately (whether he knew it or not—and he probably did not) he gave worship instead to Satan, who was behind the lies.

Science is not intrinsically evil—it is in itself a gift of God. But it is the attitude of mind that separates knowledge from God that is so dangerous and that Satan is so quick to exploit. In the vacuum that is left by our rejection of God, Satan erects an icon—most usually its outer form is our own selves, but the power lying behind is very different—and it is to that that we give worship, under the illusion that we are 'in control'. It is the downward spiral of disaster that alerts us to the inadequacy of this view.

However, the attack launched against our society has not stopped here. And for those who have rejected this worldview precisely because of its spiritual sterility, Satan has been quick to provide an alternative. Whether by means of pseudo-Eastern mysticism, or drugs, or even an unhealthy interest in magic and the occult, he has polluted some of our finest young minds and opened them up to demonic control by adulterated spirituality . . . and so many have been powerless to resist, because we have been fed the lie that all supernatural beings, which includes angels and demons, do not exist. Most terrible of all, in the church we have colluded in this lie—even though it is a view that is directly contrary to Scripture.

The term *angel* comes from a Greek word meaning messenger, and is itself a translation of the Hebrew *mal'akh*, originally meaning 'shadow side of God', but which later came to take on more specifically the sense of its Greek translation. The Old Testament does not say much about the nature of angels. In fact, to learn about the origins of angelic lore, we have to turn rather to the oldest rabbinic traditions and the later pseudepigraphical and apocryphal writings, especially the three chronicles of Enoch, compiled around the second century BC. That said, however, we do know from Scripture that from earliest times angels were seen as messengers of God, spiritual intermediaries between the wholly transcendent deity and mankind. In the first days of creation God walked with Adam and Eve in person in the garden. Even after the Fall and prior to the Flood, he met with those whose holiness of life made it possible for them to remain in his presence. Thus, in Genesis 5:22–24 we read of the patriarch Enoch: ' . . . after he became the father of Methuselah, Enoch walked with God . . . Altogether, Enoch lived 365 years. Enoch walked with God; then he was no more, because God took him away.'

However, as the increase of sin made the distance between God and man ever greater, so men and women could no longer bear his presence. God became perceived as wholly transcendent, and the belief grew that for a man or woman to come into the presence of God would mean death (cf. Jacob's profound relief at having survived his encounter with God in Genesis 32:30). So, increasingly, the distance was seen as bridged by intermediary spirits, who acted as God's agents in the government of the universe. There is no suggestion that God created the angels following on the Fall for this purpose. From the beginning it would appear that angels occupied their own sphere within creation. But, as the material world became spoiled by the entry of corruption—caused by one of these self-same spiritual beings—so the world could not bear God's naked presence without destruction, so to angels was devolved the role of implementing God's will.

This may sound strange to a worldview which sees God as wholly other, but early Jewish thought did not share the essentially Greek understanding of God as wholly other and impersonal. God, as he revealed himself to the Jews, was the Creator and his being unimaginable, but his will was also to be intimately involved with his creation, and he cared about every last detail of what went on (see Isaiah 55:8f.). The angels, therefore, were seen to have an increasingly important role as God's holiness and mankind's sin opened the gulf ever wider.

So, like mankind, angels are created. But whereas men and women are created as incarnate spiritual beings within the material world, angels are wholly spirit and, all things being equal, naturally inhabit the heavenly places. However, to the ancient mind, as we have just said, the supernatural and natural realms were not mutually exclusive, and not only did the supernatural underlie the natural, but it was felt that there was constant contact and interaction between the two.

In the earliest scriptural writings there is actually no clear distinction made between angels and God. Angels are so wholly God's mouthpiece that where they are acting as his functionaries, there is total identification of being, even though angels remain at all times subordinate spiritual entities. Thus, when the angel appears to Moses in the burning bush, he identifies himself by the words: 'I am the God of your father, the God of Abraham, the God of Issac and the God of Jacob' (Exodus 3:6). The angel therefore speaks *for* God and, as such, is of a higher order of being than mankind, because he has come from God's presence and sees God face to face—something men and women cannot, in their present state, do and survive (cf. Genesis 16:13–14).

At the same time, in the Old Testament, God is frequently given the title 'Yahweh Sabaoth', Lord of the spirits (or hosts), and we have already seen that he is pictured as presiding over a heavenly court (eg, Job 1:6; 2:1f; Psalm 89:7, etc). What goes on in this court has clear implications for the destiny of men and women; decisions are made here that affect both individual wellbeing and the fate of nations (1 Kings 22:19–23) and it is these self-same spiritual beings who, at the Lord's command, implement the decisions.

God is the Creator who has created *all* things (John 1:1–3). Angels, therefore, are as much created beings as are men, women and the whole of the rest of creation. It is, however, implied in Scripture that the creation of angels predates that of men and women (Job 38:4–7). In the first instance they were uncorrupted spiritual beings under the ordinance of God, and it would appear that they performed specific tasks at God's command. However, we also know (from their actions) that they have free will. While not expressly stated in the Old Testament, it is implied in the attitude of the satan (eg, Zechariah 3:1–2) that some exercise this faculty in ways that are actually hostile towards both God and mankind. From the Old Testament, therefore, we know that some at least, given half a chance, are liable to exceed their brief. Yet even while in rebellion there is no suggestion that they pass beyond God's control. Rather, the impression is that they have a measure of freedom within their alloted task, but there are bounds which they must not exceed.

This is important to our subject because, although a very different picture does undeniably emerge in the New Testament, there is a vital spiritual truth here that we are sometimes in danger of forgetting. The extent of Satan's hostility and rebellion is revealed in the New Testament, and alongside of that the activity of the unholy fallen spirits who have given him their allegiance; but at all times he and they cannot act outside of God's permission. Unrepented sin will give the devil a hold over our lives and a way in, which he will be quick to exploit. Yet sometimes from Scripture we know that things happen for which there is no 'legal' cause (as for instance witnessed by the temptations endured by Jesus himself, and his 'innocent' crucifixion). However, these things can only happen by God's permission, and he will allow nothing that will not work to his glory and our ultimate good. It is simply not true that if we can manage the totally impossible feat of living sinless lives, no evil or upset for the period of this life will ever befall us. The prosperity gospel is and always has been a fallacy. On the contrary, as we draw closer to God, so we will find ourselves increasingly the target of attack. Yet, once we are under the lordship of Christ, everything will work to our good (cf. Romans 8:28).

While we are on the subject of angelic rebellion and fall, it should be noted that nowhere in either Testament is it ever even so much as hinted at that the fall of angelic beings came about as the result of temptation. This means that their rebellion is self-generated, and all the worse because of that. Adam and Eve fell because they succumbed to external pressure, but from the earliest traditions it would appear that Lucifer achieved his fall all by himself, and that his rebellion stemmed initially from pride. He wanted the worship that rightfully belonged to God. And that remains his aim, and that of his minions, even today.

To gain a fuller idea of the nature and role of these beings, we need to look at Scripture in rather more detail, to see exactly what it is that angels do.

Angelic activities

The impression given in the Bible is that angels perform specific tasks. We have already seen that the satan appears to be a divinely appointed office (see Chapter 4), albeit performed with rather too much zeal. We have also seen that angels carry the messages of God. Such messages can vary tremendously in character. They can, for example, be of encouragement (Genesis 21:17), rebuke (2 Kings 1:3–4) or even announcement as, for example, when the angel Gabriel appears to Mary to tell her she is going to give birth to a son (Luke 1:26). They can also, as we have seen above, be deceitful, as when the Lord, in his wrath, sends out a lying spirit, so that men will suffer the disaster to which their choices have been leading them (see 1 Kings 22:22–23). This is to develop the idea put forward by Paul in Romans that God gives over to sin those who are sinning, even to the extent (in his wrath) of darkening their understanding, so that they are no longer capable by themselves of perceiving the good. The suggestion from the Kings passage is that this leading into greater darkness is performed not by demonic agency, but by God himself.

Angels help in times of trouble or difficulty (eg, Acts 12:7–10; Daniel 7:22). But not only can they provide protection and lead to safety, they will even supply food and drink where necessary (eg, 1 Kings 19:5–7). Frequently, in the Old Testament, we find them giving military assistance to Israel, when the latter are confronted by their enemies and seemingly facing certain destruction: 'That night the angel of the Lord went out and put to death a hundred and eighty-five thousand men in the Assyrian camp. When the people got up the next morning—there were all the dead bodies! So Sennacherib king of Assyria broke camp and withdrew' (2 Kings 19:35–36).

However, where the Jews have themselves sinned, this angelic help can turn and be launched against them with equally devastating effect (eg, 2 Samuel 24:15-17). The linchpin is at all times obedience to God. When the Jews stay faithful to God's purposes, then they are assured of divine protection and the angels fight on their behalf. But when they turn from that obedience and fall into sin, angelic help is not merely withdrawn, but actually becomes operative against them. It is their attitude that is at all times the key.

Again, there is an important lesson for us here today. We talk so much about spiritual warfare and the battle between God and evil, and this is clearly right. For those who serve God, attack and conflict are inevitable—as the Israelites themselves found, set as they were in the middle of hostile nations, and constantly under threat of attack. But when once we know Christ, our obedience ensures total protection because God himself fights on our behalf and sends his angels to our aid. The time to worry is when we step outside of that obedience. This not only weakens our defence structure, but God himself may turn against us *to recall us to himself*. Fear (in the sense of awe) of the Lord is the beginning of wisdom (Proverbs 9:10). Nowhere perhaps do we see more clearly angels being used 'to smite evildoers' at God's command than in the story of the destruction of Sodom and Gomorrah in Genesis 19. There two angels have been expressly sent to destroy the cities because of the terrible evil taking place within their walls.

Angels, therefore, can be warlike beings, but they also have their gentler side, and as well as being sent by God to encourage and announce things of great importance, there are also ministering angels whose task it is purely to give comfort. Thus, Jesus, after his power encounter with Satan in the wilderness after his baptism, is tended and restored by angels (Matthew 4:11).

A further interesting picture is given in the apocryphal book of Tobit. As already mentioned, this book of course does not have the same status as Scripture and so cannot be taken as doctrine, but it is nevertheless interesting, because there we see that the help and guidance of angels was regarded, in Jewish popular thought, as effective for personal situations of spiritual difficulty—even those not having such obvious cosmic importance as the trials undergone by Jesus. In this book Tobias, finding himself in a struggle with the demon Asmodeus, is helped by the angel Raphael:

> Tobias recalled what Raphael had told him; he took the fish's liver and heart out of the bag in which he kept them, and put them on the smoking incense. The smell from the fish held the demon off, and he took flight into upper Egypt; and Raphael instantly followed him there, and bound him hand and foot (Tobit 8:2–3).

We find an important principle of spiritual warfare illustrated here, because the demon is dealt with on the physical plane by Tobias' obedience to what has been revealed to him, but the actual binding of the demon is carried out by Raphael himself. Both actions were needed. Yet Raphael's role extends beyond that, because later in chapter 12 he tells Tobit, Tobias' father:

> When you and Sarah prayed, it was I who brought your prayers into the glorious presence of the Lord; and so too whenever you buried the dead. That day when you got up from your dinner without hesitation to bury the corpse, I was sent to test you; and again God sent me to cure both you and Sarah your daughter-in-law at the same time. I am

Raphael, one of the seven angels who stand in attendance on the Lord and enter his glorious presence (Tobit 12:12–15, NEB).

Raphael's intermediary role here has been two-way, both acting on behalf of God to man, but also representing man to God. He has apparently interceded on Tobit's and Sarah's behalf, and in response he has been sent both to test and cure, at the same time dealing with the demonic presence that is causing trouble.

Here the angel has not just revealed his presence spiritually but has actually, for a period of time, taken on human form. Of course, we find this idea in Scripture too (cf. Genesis 19:1ff.; Hebrews 13:2), but even when angels are active, men and women are not always aware of their presence. In Numbers 22:21–35, for instance, it is not Balaam but his ass who is first aware of the angel barring the way, and Balaam only realises it after the Lord himself takes pity on him and opens his eyes. So it is not always given to us to see when angels are about, nor what they are up to. However, for all that, the teaching of Scripture is that we should not discount their presence, but accept them as powerful aids.

Scripture of course talks of both good and bad angels. In the Old Testament we have suggestions of the satan going beyond his role (eg, Job 1:9–12). Equally, the appearance of Satan, the angel accuser in Zechariah 3, suggests implacable hostility towards mankind. But these were angels who, it could be said, were simply exercising their role with rather too much zeal. It is only in the New Testament that we find explicit reference to angelic beings actively working against God, under the command of the chief adversary himself—Lucifer, the fallen cherub.

However, the picture we have in the New Testament only really becomes explicable when set against the background of rabbinic myth, because so many of the traditions given expression there underlie what is accepted as virtually axiomatic by both New Testament writers and Jesus himself. For example, in 1 Corinthians 11:10, Paul gives one of the reasons why a woman should keep her head covered as being 'because of the angels'. This rather strange remark is actually a straight reference back to the seduction of women by angels referred to earlier, which gave rise to the birth of the monstrous giants, the Nephilim (Genesis 6). One strand of thought at least in rabbinic tradition stated that it was the beauty of the women's long hair that had brought about the angels' downfall. Paul is therefore anxious that women should not be a source of temptation to these spiritual beings.

Actually this is rather a strange tradition, because angels in general were not thought to be able to reproduce, and canonical literature does not delve into the differences between angelic orders. However, in the apocryphal book of Enoch 40:1–10, reference is made to an angelic order (the Watchers) that is completely unlike other angelic orders: a lesser order in fact which presumably could reproduce sexually, and which became corrupted (resulting in the fall of many of them from heaven) when they saw the daughters of Adam. An interesting aside to this tradition is that there is no indication of fallen female angelic beings in either canonical or non-canonical literature, which would presumably mean that the Watchers were seen as exclusively male. In general the higher orders of angelic beings were seen as neither male nor female—though Michael, the warrior archangel is usually portrayed as male, while Gabriel, God's messenger and co-ruler of the cherubim, is sometimes in medieval art represented as female. These representations, however, would appear to be more a product of our stereotypical attitudes of what is fitting for either sex, rather than reflecting an actual difference of gender between the angels themselves.

It is in the non-canonical myths, then, that we first find an enquiry into angelic lore. The important thing is not that we approach them with the idea of working out some kind of detailed spiritual system (which would in any case be a waste of time), but rather that we use them to understand more fully the references and thought-processes underlying Scripture, and that on that basis we come to a deeper understanding of what that means for us in spiritual terms today.

The world we live in is undeniably different from that of first-century Palestine, but our spiritual condition is actually the same, which means that Christ's victory is *the same*, and the nature of spiritual engagement is *the same*. We can try to be selective about Scripture, saying that some parts are right, and jettisoning others, but if we do that we will damage both ourselves and our relationship with God.

For centuries Christians have been selective in their approach to Scripture because they found some bits difficult to accept. Luther, for example, completely discarded any idea of there being angels, but at the same time he clung to the idea of the devil, and saw demons everywhere. At one point, in total exasperation, he even threw his ink pot at the devil, because that gentleman would not leave him alone as he was trying to write. Luther's view was such that he could see these agents of evil everywhere, and indeed frequently condemned people as being infested by demons (for example, he said of the peasants in May 1525, 'Fine Christians these! I think there is not a devil left in hell; they have all gone into these peasants.' From *Against the Robbing and Murdering Hordes of Peasants*). Nonetheless, he had no perception of help from angelic beings who were faithful to God. One can only imagine he found life rather difficult, with such an overwhelming consciousness of active evil.

Yet equally there are dangers from going too much the other way. For example, there were reports in the national press recently of an African charismatic rebel group, who claimed that they had divine protection against guns. Sadly, when it came to the crunch, the angels were not there, and they all died as they ran chanting into the oncoming fire of the frightened authorities.

We therefore need balance both in examining these myths and approaching the whole area of angelology, and above all we need humility. No one in this life will ever have a complete understanding of the nature and function of spiritual beings, but that does not mean we should over-exalt them, nor discount their existence through fear. Both attitudes are equally harmful. Over and over again we are warned in Scripture not to give worship to angels (eg, Colossians 2:18f.) but, equally, if we discount the existence of spiritual beings, our own spiritual development and understanding will be hampered. So rather, if we want to grow in spiritual maturity, we should learn what Scripture has to say, and as part of that, we should understand the underlying myths.

Hebrew myths and angelology

1. Cosmology

At the heart of Jewish faith was the belief that there was one God who had created all things in heaven and on the earth. That said, the ancient Jews viewed the universe as a hierarchy. Yahweh was both the centre of that universe, and also its highest part. As Creator, he was wholly other and transcendent, and alone occupied the realm of deity.

As God began the process of creation, the different spheres and orders of creation were seen as radiating out from his presence in descending order. In ancient schemes of cosmology, opinions varied as to whether there were two, three, seven or even ten heavens, while there were thought generally to be seven earths. The heavens were seen as fixed and vaulted over the earth, one above the other, the image most generally used being that of the skins of an onion.

Schemes varied in detail, but one common view saw the lowest heaven as containing the clouds, wind, air and upper waters and the 200 angelic beings whose job it was to watch over this realm. One variation of this tradition saw it as a part of the function of angels in this heaven to combat the attack of demons and keep them from ascending to the higher heavens. Guardian angels were also thought to inhabit this heaven.

The second heaven was thought to be the place where sinners were chained in expectation of judgement. As such it was wholly dark.

The third heaven was thought to contain the Garden of Eden, which corresponded in its description to that found in Genesis. It was thought that on death the righteous went to this heaven, which was watched over by 300 angels of light, who unceasingly sang God's praises. However, somewhat surprisingly, there was thought to be a penal area in this third heaven (Gehenna), where a river of fire wound through a land of biting ice and snow, and the wicked were tortured (again by angels).

The fourth heaven was thought to be the sphere of the great stars, along with the sun and the moon. (The ancient Hebrews shared a cosmological view with their neighbours that saw the sun and moon as being drawn through the firmament by huge chariots driven by mighty angels.)

In the fifth heaven, it was believed, the fallen angels were confined. This of course differs from other major rabbinic traditions, which saw the rebellious angels as cast down to earth—but it serves also to illustrate the wide variety of thought. Whatever, all the traditions agree that a number of angels rebelled and fell, and that their final judgement is yet to come. This fifth heaven, then, is a realm of despair.

Above that, in the sixth heaven, it was believed that seven phoenixes and seven cherubim sang God's praises without cease (another variation says they left off at dawn of each day for a short period, so that the sound of Israel's praises could rise to God). A huge number of other angels were also thought to inhabit this realm, among them the 'dominions', known in Hebrew as the *hashmallim*, and the 'powers', also variously named the *dynamios*, potentiates and authorities. These mighty angels were believed to be among the first angels created by God, and their main activity was seen as in the perilous border regions between the first and second heavens—perilous because it was believed that it was in that heavenly place that the battle was fought out for demonic control of the earth. Paul also warned that these powers could be both good and evil (Romans 13:1), their battleground being that of the human soul. We shall return to this in Chapter 10, in the section dealing with principalities and powers.

The seventh, or highest, heaven was believed to be inhabited by God himself. It was a realm filled with ineffable light, and there God occupied his divine throne, surrounded by the seven archangels, the cherubim and seraphim, and the divine wheels or thrones (on which last it was believed that God rode when he left his heavenly throne: eg, Ezekiel 10:9–17). In this highest heaven, it was thought that these angelic beings ceaselessly sang God's praises—and one line of tradition at least saw these angels as being involved with God in the song of creation.

These seven heavens were seen as attached to the seven earths by huge hooks which prevented it all from falling apart and dropping into the void. It was believed that every day God mounted on one of the divine wheels or thrones (actually a separate angelic order and not an object) and, driven by a cherub, visited all his worlds.

2. Angels

Angels, as wholly spiritual beings, were thus believed in common Jewish thought to stand closer to God than men and women and to inhabit the heavens, which, as we have seen, were themselves hierarchically ordered. Matter and flesh, being subject to decay, were seen as distant from the transcendent, eternally unchanging and incorporeal reality of God. Men and women therefore inhabited the world, which was a fairly low order of creation. However, they stood out as distinct from the rest of the created order in that, together and jointly, they were made in the image of God and contained the breath of God (Genesis 1:26f.). Prior to the Fall, of course, they too enjoyed the privilege of walking with God, and their especial task, as well as living in that direct eternal relationship with God, was to care for the created order—which was initially located, in the above scheme, in the third heaven.

Men and women, therefore, had enormous potential, and in their redeemed state it was thought that they would one day stand even over the angels in judgement, as attested to by Paul (1 Corinthians 6:3). However, unredeemed, it was all too patently clear that humanity was inferior to the angels. Rabbinic traditions (echoed by Job) testify to their creation prior to that of men and women, and they were clearly used by God in his governance of the world. We have already examined, for example, the tradition that testifies to Lucifer's appointment as guardian cherub of this world—a position of pre-eminence which, it was believed, fuelled his pride and led directly to his rebellion. From these traditions, then, although angels did not naturally inhabit the material world, they could and did interact with it, and were indeed an essential part of maintaining its right order. Therefore, while men and women, at God's express command, physically ruled over the earth, at the supernatural level, the angels were charged with its care—and, it must be concluded, with the care too of men and women.

The tradition relating to the fall of the archangel Samael (in the rabbinic traditions, as we have seen, an alternative candidate for Satan) is of particular interest here, because it relates how Samael became jealous when he first saw Adam and objected vehemently when God told the host of heaven to worship his new creation. While all the others bowed the knee, Samael apparently refused because, he said, Adam had been created after him and so was quite patently a lesser being and did not, therefore, deserve worship. It may be remembered that at this point, the archangel Michael intervened and told him to beware. But Samael by this point had stirred up a group of similarly minded malcontents, and they refused. Samael somewhat unwisely said that if God 'showed anger', he would set up his own throne above the stars and proclaim himself sovereign. Not surprisingly this provoked a reaction from his enraged counterpart, and Michael threw him down to earth. Once confined there, so the tradition runs, Samael became the guiding force behind an organised opposition which, from that point on, actively began to work against God's will.

This is an interesting tradition and, though bearing many points of similarity to the Lucifer tradition, clearly differs in certain important aspects—most importantly of course in that the Lucifer traditions see a clear delegation of authority to the archangel who, though he abuses his position, is clearly initially placed as prince over this world. I believe the Lucifer tradition more effectively explains the intensely legal character of so much spiritual warfare—the insistence on 'right' of occupation that is cancelled only by Christ's blood.

Despite these extremely early rabbinic traditions, the Old Testament by and large does not draw a distinction between good and bad angels. However, in Daniel (10:10–14), when the angel finally breaks through to the prophet in response to his prayer, he gives as the reason for his apparent delay in responding the fact that he has had to do battle with the prince of Persia, and only succeeded in breaking through when Michael, the prince of Israel, came to his aid. This accords with the early Jewish belief (shared with that of other peoples round about) that every nation had been appointed a guardian spirit. Here, the prince/angel of Persia is clearly hostile to Israel. Israel was believed to be God's chosen nation, the one people the Lord had reserved to himself, following on the Fall, so that they might in time become the instrument of redemption. The implication therefore is clearly that whereas the angel of Israel is 'good', the angel of Persia is 'bad', because he is opposing God (see Chapter 10 for a fuller discussion of principalities).

So while rabbinic tradition told of a rebellion in heaven, and of an angelic fall *prior* to that of Adam and Eve, the same traditions inform us that different orders of angels were believed to fall into distinct groups, which in turn determined their function. The bottom line was that angels—at whatever level—were created to worship and wait upon God. The highest grouping or order within this celestial hierarchy was the *seraphim*. As we have seen, it was believed that they occupied the seventh heaven, ceaselessly chanting God's praises while circling the divine throne. They clearly exist to glorify and 'guard' God, and they would also appear to be moral beings: Michael, for example, is referred to as a seraph, and so too is Gabriel (though both also of course have other functions, which we will examine below), but Lucifer is also said to have been a seraph prior to his fall.

In the Old Testament the seraphs appear and are described in detail in Isaiah 6:2. There they stand above God as he sits enthroned in the temple (the sign of his presence in Israel). Each has six wings; with two they cover their face, with two they cover their feet, and with two they fly. They are recorded as singing the trisagion:

> Holy, holy, holy is the Lord of hosts;
> The whole earth is full of his glory.

The effect of this powerful praise is to shake the foundations of the building, and fill the whole temple with smoke.

Ranking immediately beneath the seraphim, were thought to come the *cherubim*. There are far more frequent references to this order in Scripture than to the seraphim, and they generally appear to be far more war-like in character. It is the cherubim, for instance, whom God stations at the east of Eden, giving to them the ever-turning, flaming sword with which to guard the tree of life (Genesis 3:24). In Ezekiel 10 they are represented as 'driving' God's throne, and their image was physically placed at either end of the Ark of the Covenant as a sign of their divine protection. Solomon also scattered carvings and images of the cherubim throughout the Temple when it was built in Jerusalem, and some of them appear to have been absolutely huge in size (see 2 Chronicles 3·7–14).

Overall, then, they are far more of a warrior group than the seraphim (although there would appear to be some overlap) and in Revelation, when Michael appears at the head of the angels, it is most probably the cherubim who make up the forces under his command. Interestingly, both Babylonian and Sumeriam myth have the same fabulous and terrible winged creatures whose function it was to guard temples and holy places (the *Ka-ri-bu*). In Babylon they would probably have stood as guard at the entrance to the Temple, and the Jews would most certainly have come across these creatures during their captivity. But, as we know from their portrayal in the earliest non-canonical traditions, they were already well-established in Jewish thought long before that time.

As we have seen above, there are a variety of rabbinic traditions describing the composition of the heavens. The comparatively late Chronicles of Enoch also deserve mention here, because in them the scribe describes his journey through 'the ten heavens'. What is most interesting is that he relates in great detail his encounters with the angels he finds at each level, but although he comes across some 'bad' angels, he does not have any single level corresponding to hell or the abyss (cf. above, where both the second and fifth heavens are seen as specific punishment areas, while more specifically Gehenna is located in the third heaven, north of Eden). What Enoch does have, at and within each one of the various levels, is a clearly delineated and rather terrible punishment area, ruled over by angels of punishment, who most definitely are obedient to God.

Enoch, however, is unique (as well as being comparatively late). More usually the traditions locate 'hell' (the place into which stroppy angels are cast) in the outer reaches of creation, *below* the earth. Whatever line is followed, however, it is abundantly clear that angels are seen as all too capable of transgression, and that it is not only men and women who have the ability to sin. This is interesting, because it implies not redemption on a cosmic scale (at no point is the redemption of these fallen angels even hinted at, however obscurely) but a cosmic cleansing tied to the redemption of creation. However, Scripture is very clear that this last will not happen until God has cleansed the created order and, though the battle is to be fought out in the heavenly places, there is parallel expression upon the earth. This is important, because again it expresses the close tie between the natural and supernatural that was thought to exist from earliest times in Jewish thought.

It is important for us too today because, despite the fact that at this time our cultural worldview is so exclusively material, the Bible teaches that the battle in which we are engaged extends far beyond its manifest form—indeed, it is in the spiritual realm that the battle is actually fought, and the natural simply follows what has already taken place in the supernatural realm. Therefore, the lesson for us is that problems must be tackled at both levels, because we will never see any lasting physical and material change if the spiritual problem is not addressed first. (Equally, of course, we shall not see any lasting change if the spiritual side alone is tackled and nothing is done in practical terms to remedy the situation.) This is as true for social, political and cultural conditions as it is for our own health and well-being. Effective ministry follows and implements what is happening in the spiritual realm. In this we follow God—which means that we have God's authority. But, perhaps even more importantly, when our personal relationship with God is right, then the conditions of our life fall into place, and God brings order out of what can appear to be total chaos. The material or natural is the outward form of the spiritual or supernatural.

A young couple came up to me after a meeting

recently (I shall call them Margaret and Bob) and asked for prayer. They told me that they had been trying for a number of years to have a baby, but without success. They were both healthy, in their early thirties, but Margaret had been totally unable to conceive. As we talked I kept feeling God prompting me about their work situation, and especially in relation to Margaret. What I felt God saying was that there was not any real 'problem', but that she would not conceive until the spiritual and outward conditions of their life together were right. I did not feel that this was in any sense 'punishment', but rather a demonstration of God's love for them, because if they were to have a baby at that time, living the way they were, they would not be able to cope.

Now I should stress that I knew absolutely nothing about Margaret and Bob prior to this conversation. This was the first time we had met and I knew nothing about their lives, but I told them my thoughts because they seemed relevant. As the couple listened they looked at each other, and then Bob said, 'You can't know this, but we're both looking for new jobs at the moment. Margaret works up north and is away all week, and we've been trying to find jobs where we can be together without all this separation.' It felt like a real encouragement and a promise from God (and I'm waiting now to hear what happens!). But I believe that the key point here is that God wanted them to be in the right material conditions to have a child, so that they and their relationship would not be damaged spiritually!

More usually, of course, things happen the other way round, and I have so often come across people with serious physical conditions, who have first needed to have their relationship with God or others 'put right' in order for them to receive healing. But I felt that God's word to this young couple was a real mark of his love for them, and showed very clearly the relationship that exists between the material and the spiritual.

10
Demons

In the New Testament, a wide variety of names is given to evil powers, including: principalities, powers, princes, gods, angels and spirits (unclean, wicked, elemental). It would seem, however, that devils and demons are separate entities. The former are fallen angels, but the latter would appear to be invisible evil spirits occupying the ethereal spaces between God and humanity. Incorporeal, their desire is to take over human beings so that they can find expression through material form. This distinction appears to be indicated in Acts 23:8–9, where we read:

> (The Sadducees say that there is no resurrection, and that there are neither angels nor spirits, but the Pharisees acknowledge them all.)
> There was a great uproar, and some of the teachers of the law who were Pharisees stood up and argued vigorously. 'We find nothing wrong with this man . . . What if a spirit or an angel has spoken to him?'

Similarly, in Revelation 16:13 we read: ' . . . I saw three evil spirits that looked like frogs; they came out of the mouth of the dragon, out of the mouth of the beast and out of the mouth of the false prophet. They are spirits of demons performing miraculous signs . . . '

In this latter context it would appear that the spirits are abominations spawned by Satan himself and as such bear his image and are involved in his work. They are called demons. But in the passage from Acts, the spirits are mentioned alongside angels and there is no particular suggestion of demonic agency at work. Indeed the Pharisees are defending Paul by asserting that there is nothing wrong if an angel or spirit has spoken to him— the implication being of divine agency working for good through both. Evil spirits are therefore demons, but it would seem equally true that there are 'good' spirits who are not demonic, but who at the same time are to be differentiated from angels. This is fascinating and points to a rich stratum of thought that we shall do our best to unpack. It is also very important, not just because there is so much talk in Christian circles today about demon-possession, but also because of the implications it has for so much New Age thought. One cannot help but think that if some of the New Agers knew what they were opening themselves up to, they would think twice before becoming involved.

Origins

Scripture does not say anything specifically about the origin of demons, so again it is instructive to look at some of the early rabbinic traditions, as well as the beliefs of some of the cultures with which Judaism came into contact—because, in this area at least, they display a similarity of worldview.

Early Jewish thought was distinctively and unusually monotheistic, but no one doubted the existence and activities of evil spirits or demons, which were seen as causing *some* forms of physical and mental illness, and as standing behind other religions antithetical to Jewish belief. However, other peoples apart from the Jews were just as much prey to unwelcome demonic attentions and, in the ancient world, the Jews were much in demand as exorcists (a role subsequently taken over by Christians) because their God was believed to be extraordinarily powerful in dealing with such troublesome things. In ancient thought, to know the name of someone was to have a measure of control over them, but no one knew Yahweh's name (it may be remembered that when Moses asked him, God responded, 'Yahweh,' which simply means 'I am who I am'). It was therefore concluded that the God of the Israelites had to be *very* powerful, because he was unknowable! This then extended to the spiritual realm. The Jewish exorcists would find out the name of the demon, and then cast it out in the name of Yahweh. It is interesting to note, on top of that, that Jesus was so powerful he did not usually bother even to enquire the name of the demon, but simply told it to go; and the demons, recognising him and the power of God that flowed from him, instantly obeyed!

Clearly the Jews must have thought about the origins of these troublesome spirits, and they came up with a variety of accounts. Now it must be emphasised before we examine these popular traditions that they are *not* scriptural. They are nevertheless interesting because they stand behind and inform the scriptural representations we have. The gospel writers, for example, would most certainly have been aware of them, as would Jesus himself. To know them is then, I believe, to have a greater understanding of Scripture; but they should not be relied upon as revelation. Having said this, let us examine in more detail some of these myths.

One tradition says that when God first created Adam he was lonely and begged God to create for him a mate. God responded by creating for him the first woman, Lilith. But whereas he had created Adam out of the dust, he formed Lilith from the sediment and filth, with unfortunate results. Lilith sprang to life as a demoness. Adam mated with her (and with Naamah, another demoness, whose precise origins remain tantalisingly obscure) and from their union was born Asmodeus (the demon we have already encountered in the story of Tobit), along with innumerable lesser demons, all of whom have, from that moment on, plagued humanity.

As might have been expected, the relationship between Adam and Lilith ran into difficulties—in particular she objected to Adam's trying to force her to lie in the subordinate position when they were mating. She therefore ran off to the Red Sea, where she discovered many 'lascivious demons' and bore them hundreds of demon offspring—the *lilim*. She escaped the curse of death because she left Adam long before he succumbed to temptation, and so has survived as a very powerful female demon. As late as the Middle Ages, Lilith was thought to strangle babies and to seduce dreaming men (monks especially were felt to be the object of her attentions). Even today she is a powerful figure in the occult and magic.

A second line of tradition sees demons as the unnatural offspring produced by the union of angels and women referred to in Genesis 6. The sons of God, the tradition runs, were sent to teach men and women truth and justice, but fell when they began themselves to lust after the women they had been sent to teach. Among their number were two angels in particular, Shemhazai and Azael. Shemhazai subsequently repented, but Azael did not, and he taught women the use of cosmetics and ornaments and how, in turn, to seduce men. God was so incensed that he sent the Flood to cleanse the earth of such wickedness, and to destroy the *nephilim* (the name given to their offspring). At the same time he sent the archangel Raphael to bind Azael hand and foot and imprison him in a cave until the last judgement. It is interesting to note that on the Day of Atonement, the sins of the nation having been ritually heaped onto the head of the scapegoat, it was then thrown over the cliff to Azazel . . . 'as some call Azael', from which we can conclude that this fallen angel has remained a powerful figure in Jewish thought.

Throughout the rest of the ancient world, however, *daimones* (as the spirit forces were known) occupied a rather different position. The worldview of the ancients was profoundly religious. This was as true, for example, of the Mayans, the followers of Brahma, the Druids and the Canaanites, to name but a few, as it was for the Jews. Whatever their ethnic origins, people saw the spirit world as closely bound with our own. We see this reflected not only in the many and diverse forms of cultic worship, but also in the keen interest in astrology and use of magic. There was a common belief that through the correct use of formulae, people could not only know the future, but could in some way even gain control over the spirits or gods, and so influence what happened in life.

Spirits were seen then as very powerful. To the pagans they were the rather ambiguous intermediaries who stood between gods and men . . . spiritual deputies for the gods, almost. And like the gods, they could be highly unpredictable. Their support needed to be wooed, and while some would give favour and protection to men and women, others could be capricious and some downright obstructive. As a general principle, those who had been appointed to specific tasks by the gods were felt to be good, but the ancient mind, while in general eschewing the idea of an organised kingdom of evil, acknowledged that there could be rogue spirits who acted outside of any remit of the gods, and who left a trail of chaos in their path. It was recognised that the influence of such spirits could be malign, and that where they had got a hold, it could be broken only by the use of powerful spells.

Influence on humans

Yet it was believed that there was a further dimension to the activities of these spirits, and we see it perhaps most clearly articulated in Greek and Roman thought. The Greeks, for example, believed that every man and woman had his or her own attendant *daimon*, who presided over the day of birth, and from that point on acted as a kind of guiding power. Similarly, the Romans believed that every man and woman had an attendant *genius*, born with the individual and exercising a similar function to its Greek counterpart. As a rider to this belief, individuals would not infrequently commune with their attendant spirits. Thus, for instance, the Roman writer Horace claimed that he was attended by the powerful woodland god Pan, who visited him often when he was down on his farm, and gave him protection and advice. But, though perhaps most clearly expressed in Greek and Roman belief systems, the idea of attendant spirits was by no means limited to these cultures, and in India, for example, we find that Brahma also claimed to be attended by a huge number of ministering spirits or demons.

Daimones, then, were spirit entities who, in pagan belief, could be either good or bad. An interesting point to note here, before looking at the early Christian response to these beliefs, is the Jewish belief in *guardian angels*, which goes back to long before the birth of Christ. It was believed that these angels were appointed at birth and exercised a similar function to the Greek attendant *daimon*. However, the Jews did not just believe in one attendant spirit, and the Talmud speaks specifically of every Jew being assigned 11,000 guardian angels at birth—a rather large number by any reckoning. But Jesus himself affirmed a belief in angelic protection: 'See that you do not look down on one of these little ones. For I tell you that their angels in heaven always see the face of my Father in heaven' (Matthew 18:10).

Interestingly, Christian thought developed this idea even further, and it later came to be believed by the early church that every Christian at birth was assigned two angels—one good, who sat at the right hand and led the individual in obedience, and one bad, who sat on the left and tried to nudge towards evil.

The point of interest here is that many New Agers today, following a variety of different cults, ideas and philosophies, claim to have spirit and angel guides. The actress Shirley Maclaine, for example, has done much to promote the idea of 'channelling' in the United States (communication with higher intelligences and spirits who give directions that they claim will help both the individual and the world). In Scotland, the New Age community at Findhorn claims to be in touch with and guided by nature spirits, in particular the god Pan, who, they claim, regularly manifests himself. These are perhaps extreme examples, but many people today, even on the fringes of New Age thought, will claim belief in spirit guidance. I do not believe they should be dismissed as 'loony'. They have in fact opened themselves up to a very real spiritual power, and this power is unquestionably demonic. The battle for the soul is as much a reality today as it was in first-century Palestine . . . And that brings us back to the attitude of the early church in response to these Greek and Roman ideas, and in particular to the writings of the apologists.

The views of the apologists

Justin Martyr was one of the first early Christian writers to take over and expound the teaching of the church on angels. In particular, he subscribed to the belief that demons were the offspring of fallen angels and women. It was the work of these demons now, he said, to try and blind men and women to the truth as revealed in Christ, and so keep them enslaved to Satan. In particular, he argued that demons worked mischief by healing and occasionally predicting the future, and he rejected any apparent similarities between Christian and pagan worship or myth as a clever counterfeit of the truth inspired by the devil, with the aim of diverting worship from the true God.

Lest it be assumed at this point that Justin dismissed everything not specifically Christian as demonic, it should be pointed out that he fiercely defended the God-given gift of reason, which, while not perhaps all too obviously allied to faith of any kind, was, he maintained, a divine spark implanted by God to keep men and women alert to truth, until that time when the truth became incarnate in Jesus and redemption then became possible. Justin therefore drew a clear distinction between what was demonically inspired, and what was outside of that influence, although not capable in itself of becoming a means of salvation. Again, this is important for us today. Justin then saw it as an important part of his task to distinguish between the spirits.

In similar fashion Origen found a bridge between the pagan and Christian worlds by route of the Graeco-Roman cosmological view referred to above; that is, the view that saw the world as subject to the guardianship of spirits, the *daimones*. Not true, Origen said. The *daimones* existed, but far from being good, they were evil spirits, who exercised their influence under the lordship of Satan. Here then we have an explicit equation drawn between *daimones* and demons, and this is going to be important in our section on principalities and powers, below.

Worship of demons

There is one further important point to be made before we move on from our discussion of demons. It has to do with the role consistently assigned to them from earliest times in Scripture. The ancient Hebrews believed that all worship offered to foreign deities and idols was in fact being offered to demons, and that was a view they consistently maintained right up to the time of Christ, when it was taken over and similarly forcibly articulated by the earliest New Testament writers. In Leviticus 17:7 we read: 'They [the Jews] must no longer offer any of their sacrifices to the goat idols [demons] to whom they prostitute themselves. This is to be a lasting ordinance for them and for the generations to come.'

Similarly in Deuteronomy 32:17, one of the charges brought against Israel is: 'They sacrificed to demons, which are not God—gods they had not known, gods that recently appeared, gods your fathers did not fear.'

Paul is equally explicit in his view that behind the pagan idols, in themselves nothing, are powerful demons. He says that you cannot take part in this demon worship and be a Christian too.

> Do I mean then that a sacrifice offered to an idol is anything, or that an idol is anything? No, but the sacrifices of pagans are offered to demons, not to God, and I do not want you to be participants with demons. You cannot drink the cup of the Lord and the cup of demons too; you cannot have a part in both the Lord's table and the table of demons (1 Corinthians 10:19–21).

Many Christians today are blithely following practices they have taken over from all sorts of other religious traditions. Many are also following a hotchpotch of New Age teachings in the mistaken belief that this will not damage their faith. They are wrong. Paul is quite explicit that behind these practices are demons, and we simply cannot give worship both to demons and God. It does not matter that we may simply join in these things out of politeness and without any committed belief. In themselves, Paul says, these things cannot harm us and do not hold power over us, because Christ has broken their power. But it is no longer appropriate to put ourselves in that position of offering worship when once we have claimed to come under the lordship of Christ, nor is it right for us to suggest to others by our conduct that worship offered to such things is either right or good.

To that I would add that we actually expose ourselves to enormous spiritual damage if we take part in things that have behind them demonic power. On the one hand, we actually open ourselves up to that demonic influence—we invite it into our lives, and the devil is quick to take us up on the invitation. On the other hand, if at some point we have actually made a genuine commitment to God, from that moment on a very real battle begins to take place. So, if we participate in such things, first of all we become subject to God's wrath, because we are doing something he has expressly forbidden and, second, where the devil perceives the movement of our spirit, he too will try and attack, because he hates and despises any commitment to God. So we may well find that all sorts of unpleasant things start to happen in our lives, ranging from sickness, to relationship problems, to a total disruption of work.

Similarly, if we make a half-hearted movement towards God, having previously been involved in these things, we can find ourselves in for a rough ride as a real battle for our soul gets under way. Where this is happening, the person needs to seek help from someone of spiritual maturity whom they can trust, and tremendous discernment is needed, because almost certainly what is being experienced will be a combination of the two. God's wrath is actually wonderful and a tremendous sign of his love, and needs repentance. The devil's attack needs standing against in the authority of Christ and must be rebuked. As it says in James 4:7, 'Submit yourselves, then, to God. Resist the devil, and he will flee from you.' A wrong perception may only exacerbate the problem.

In an earlier book, *No Other Gods*, I wrote of my own involvement in Transcendental Meditation. I can most certainly testify to the problems of opening up to this kind of hold, and it was entirely by God's grace that I was freed. In recent years my ministry has come increasingly to be what I describe as a ministry of freedom and release. I find myself working more and more with people who have been damaged or bound in some way as a result of their involvement in things that are unhelpful, or even things done to them. It has been God who has brought these people and this ministry to me. And it is this God-given ministry that has given birth to Anastasis (the group with which I currently work).

I would like to say, by way of encouragement, that the difficulties have not stopped, but they have changed radically. There have been difficulties that I and my family have not been able to avoid—attacks on health, attacks on reputation, attacks through accident, attacks by way of violent response sometimes when I stand up and talk at a meeting. I once imagined that when you were serving God in obedience, all the problems would cease, but the Lord has shown me a different way. For all of us our path is different and this will not be true for everyone. But I would like to say this for those labouring under a terrible burden of undefined guilt, and for those who are experiencing problems and have been repenting of everything till they are blue in the face, and yet still they cannot break free. The Lord has shown me that obedience of heart is the key, but he has shown me too that I and my family are the object of attack precisely because we are committed to his will. More than anything else in recent months, he has shown me how he was attacked in his life upon earth, and how he resisted. But he has shown me too how he stands in protection around us, and how because of that we have absolutely nothing to fear. And through all of this he has taught me the way of praise, and of love, as a weapon. Praise is not just about feeling good. It is one of the most powerful weapons we have in our spiritual armoury: the demons hear and tremble.

If we pay homage to demons, then spiritually we open ourselves to enormous harm. This will have psychological consequences, but it needs dealing with spiritually for us to be free. The first and most important thing therefore is repentance. But then we need to grow in the freedom of Christ, and the devil will do all in his power to try and stop us from coming into that knowledge. It is when we come into that knowledge that the demons fall and the gates are shattered before us. God's power is as real today as it was in first-century Palestine in the person of Christ. The difference is that by the Holy Spirit that power is now made available to every one of us. In Christ we have new life. Purity and obedience are the keys to the exercise of God's power in the Spirit. Demons are real, and are still a power, but their power is as nothing before Christ. In the name of Christ all authority is given to us—literally—but we have to learn how to use that power in obedience to Christ. Otherwise we ourselves become guilty of trying to practise a form of magic, and find ourselves yet again giving worship to an obscurely hidden demon. God will not allow that. He will not allow the abuse of his name. If as Christians today we have lost, or have never even seen, the power of faith; if we believe that God's power is simply confined to the pages of the New Testament; if we do not expect to see miracles—then we should look to the heart of our relationship with God, and ask him to teach us the way of obedience.

Demons and angels compared

Demons do exist and are to be distinguished from fallen angels. They would appear to be lesser evil spirits, who bear the mark of Satan and serve his purposes in the world. Nevertheless, their natural habitat is 'the air' or heavenly places. True, they attempt to find expression through and within the material, but this is not their proper sphere, as we see in the gospel story of the Gerasene demoniac: the demons who had taken up residence were 'trespassing', and so Jesus simply returned them to their proper habitation. Men and women become vulnerable to their infestation either by inviting these demonic presences into their lives, or through some point of entry weakened by unrepented sin, whether personal or ancestral.

Equally there would appear to be 'good' spirits, who act as guardian angels. Whether a complete identification can be made between these spirits and guardian angels is not known, and largely irrelevant, although in Hebrews 1:14 the writer states: 'Are not all angels ministering spirits sent to serve those who will inherit salvation?'

Guardian angels and demons, then, would seem to work in opposition to each other. Whereas angels are at no point invasive and seek simply to protect, and guide the individual into closer relationship to God, demons seek to control and find expression for their own personalities through men and women where they are vulnerable to infestation (which basically means in areas not submitted to the lordship and thus protection of God). In this sense demons are parasitic, and tend to group together. They would also appear to be intensely legalistic, standing on their right of occupation through unrepented sin. However, like their lord they are already defeated and have to give way before Christ.

Powers and principalities

Many pagan cults frequently associated a particular god with a particular city. We know, for example, from the book of Acts that Ephesus was specifically linked with Artemis (Acts 19:28) and had a huge temple dedicated to her worship. The temple was located there because it was believed that the goddess gave to the people her especial favour and protection. Both her position and power were challenged by Paul as he preached the gospel, and that led directly to a riot.

We see an outworking of the same belief system in Moses' conflict with Pharaoh, as he brought out the Children of Israel from bondage in Egypt at Yahweh's express command. The battle Moses found himself engaged in actually had little to do with the popular idea of a liberation movement. This was, for example, no social and political struggle against apartheid, but was a straightforward power encounter between the gods of the Egyptians (who stood behind Pharaoh) and Yahweh himself.

By extension, it was similarly accepted throughout the ancient world that behind the ruler of the state lay his *daimon*, the powerful spiritual genius under whose influence he wielded power. Indeed, one of the ways in which kings held power and established dynasties was by claiming not just divine appointment, but divine status. In Egypt, for example, Amenophis IV, who followed the cult of Aten (the Solar Disc), changed his name in the god's honour to Akhenaten (the splendour of Aten). He proclaimed Aten to be the sole god, but at the same time he himself claimed divine status, and was worshipped as such. The political rationale behind this of course was that it was very difficult for mere mortals to challenge the power of a god: the ruler could thus try and ensure for himself a measure of both political stability and safety! However, there was clearly more behind this than simple political philosophy, and rulers were commonly identified with gods. Their health and well-being mirrored the strength of the state, while at the same time it was a part of their function, in their persons, to protect the land under their rule.

We see this kind of idea, in modified form, underlying the fate that befalls Israel when David, in direct disobedience, undertakes a census of the fighting men of Israel. As punishment Yahweh offers him three options: either three years of famine, three years of military defeat, or three years of plague, with the angel of the Lord ravaging every part of Israel. David chooses plague, but the interesting point is that the nation is punished because of *his* sin, and the punishment is ended only when, having repented, David intercedes at the Lord's direction (1 Chronicles 21:7ff.). There is clearly no suggestion of a guardian spirit at work here, fighting on Israel's behalf. The incident illustrates the way in which ancient peoples, the Jews included, accepted the belief that the ruler was divinely appointed and stood in a special relationship with the deity.

However, as we have seen, pagan cultures went even beyond this, commonly seeing their ruler as not just appointed, but as the physical incarnation of a ruling god. We have therefore in antiquity two widely accepted ideas. First, that behind the ruler stood the gods and that the ruler exercised power by divine mandate and direction; and second, that the ruler was the physical manifestation of the divine power that had the nation in care.

In rabbinic angelology we find an interesting counterpart to these ideas which underlie both references in Daniel and some otherwise inexplicable ideas to be found in the New Testament. We have already seen that ancient Jewish thought believed that there were many subordinate spirits under God's sovereignty. One specific order of angels was believed to be *the principalities*. These angels were seen as appointed to the charge of the nations and great cities on earth. We first find specific reference to this belief in Deuteronomy 32:8: When the Most High gave the nations their inheritance, when he divided all mankind, he set up boundaries for the peoples *according to the number of the sons of God (bene elohim)*' (italics mine).

In Daniel we find reference to *the prince of the Persian kingdom*, who tries to prevent the angel who has been dispatched in response to Daniel's prayer from reaching him, and is defeated only with the aid of Michael (Daniel 10:4–14). Again, it is probably this same belief that underlies the reference in the apocryphal book Ecclesiasticus, where we find it stated: 'For every nation he appointed a ruler, but chose Israel to be his own possession' (17:17, NEB).

This last can, of course, be read as a straight reference to the appointment of an earthly ruler, but the interesting point to note is that in the Daniel passage, the hostile angel of Persia is simply called *the king of Persia*. There would seem therefore to be identification between the angel given charge of the nation and his earthly counterpart, which echoes the pagan belief already alluded to, that behind every earthly ruler stood his attendant *daimon*.

We may therefore conclude from all this that the Jews believed that God had assigned specific angels as tutelary deities to the nations, but that he had reserved Israel to his own especial care, appointing as their angelic prince (as we know from Daniel 10:12–13, 20–21) the great archangel Michael himself.

Throughout the Old Testament we are aware of a constant struggle between Israel and 'the nations'. In worldly terms this is hardly surprising, because geographically Israel was tiny, and yet it occupied land that was both fertile and crucial to the balance of power throughout the ancient Near East. With the balance constantly shifting between Egypt and Assyria, Israel, in the centre of the campaign route, was a prime target for invasion, quite apart from the expansionist pretensions of these major empires. Added to that, Israel's original political system, being based on, as it is thought, no more than a loose confederation of tribes held together by a common belief in Yahweh, was hardly best suited to maintaining independence in face of the aggressive nature of the major military powers that surrounded them. And yet Israel's victory or defeat is never presented as dependent on military prowess. Rather, the fortunes of its people are seen as inextricably linked to the purity of their faith, and their obedience to Yahweh. When the people are obedient, then God himself fights for them, but when they turn from him, following the religious practices of the nations that surround them and attempting to rely on their own political and military expertise for security, then God withdraws that protection and disaster follows. 'If my people would but listen to me, if Israel would follow my ways, how quickly would I subdue their enemies and turn my hand against their foes!' (Psalm 81:13–14).

Spiritually the rationale is clear. The conflict Israel found itself at the centre of actually had nothing to do with nationalist pretensions, but was in fact an outworking of the struggle between God and the gods—the fallen angels who stood behind these other nations and maintained power by masquerading as gods.

It was not a question of these other gods being as powerful as Yahweh. At no point was God's sovereignty ever in question. And, while Israel maintained obedience, though they might be frequently attacked, nothing could actually touch them and victory was assured. The lesson for Israel was to learn that obedience. It is exactly the same scenario that we have already seen in Moses' confrontation with Pharaoh—a spiritual battle in which the outcome is never in doubt. God permits the exercise of Pharaoh's authority and the seeming 'defeats' only in order that the absolute nature of his power be demonstrated.

The picture we have, then, is of fallen angels ('princes') who give their allegiance to Satan, standing behind the nations and foreign religious cults. However, although they exercise an illegitimate authority over the earth, they are still firmly located under the sovereignty of God.

In the charismatic wing of the church today, much is said about ruling powers and principalities, and the criticism is frequently made that there is little biblical foundation for it. I would disagree with this. It is a belief underlying the worldview of both Old and New Testament writers. And the brief references we have in

Scripture are not fleshed out precisely because it was an accepted part of their thought. The angels who governed the nations, apart from Israel, were seen as having become implicated in the Fall. But God reserved Israel to himself in order that he might, in time, bring about the redemption of the whole of creation. To this end, he appointed the powerful archangel Michael (who was loyal) as prince of Israel . . . precisely because he had in mind from the beginning to make that nation the chosen instrument of his redemption (eg, Daniel 12:1f.).

In Revelation we are told that at the Fall, Satan took one third of the angels with him (12:4). From elsewhere in Scripture (eg, Isaiah 14) it would appear that at least some of these angels were the tutelary spirits who had been appointed to special positions of care over the nations. It is impossible to say if their number includes all the angels/princes who had been appointed to care for the nations. However, it would seem, as for example in Isaiah 14, that the ruler/nation took on the characteristics of the angelic guardian power that stood behind it. In this passage, for example, though it is the king of Babylon who is being talked about, the picture merges almost imperceptibly into that of Lucifer, who stands behind. The king is wholly controlled by Satan—his pride and pretensions are satanic. Both aspire to mount the throne of assembly and win for themselves the position of glory that rightly belongs only to God. In fact, the king has so wholly identified with his angelic overlord, whose instrument he has become, that he no longer has separate existence. This, then, is a powerful expression of the belief that behind the nations of the ancient world stood powerful spiritual forces, which were clearly influential in human destiny. But, at the same time, the Jews believed that these angelic overlords were completely under the control of God. They may be hostile to him, as demonstrated by the constant threat that hung over Israel, but they could not act outside of his permission, and they lacked his power.

There are important lessons from all of this. First, we need to take seriously the spiritual realities underlying world structures and events. This does not mean that we should automatically see all worldly powers and institutions as evil. Paul himself points out that all rulers are ultimately appointed by God: 'Everyone must submit himself to the governing authorities, for there is no authority except that which God has established. The authorities that exist have been established by God' (Romans 13:1). Nevertheless, given that, we should recognise that at least some of those 'spiritual' appointments may well be hostile to God and that just as within the human soul there is a battle, so too in worldly structures there is a struggle for possession. Satan's basic aim is to usurp the position that rightfully belongs to God, and that means nothing lies outside of his attempted operations. Where a nation, structure or institution is not consciously submitted to God, it will be susceptible to the deceits of Satan. Where it falls, it can become a tool for Satan.

We see this, for example, in what happened under the Nazis during the Second World War. The conventional picture we have of the German character is as proud and self-disciplined. However, the problem in the 1930s-40s was that the German people became caught by the lure of world domination. This clearly was a satanic deception, similar to that which brought about the fall of the Babylonian king referred to in Isaiah. That lure was closely linked to their pride; by succumbing, they opened themselves up to the outworking and control of far greater evil.

I believe we see the same pattern and potentiality in every organisation and human structure. This is not to suggest that every organisation has a ruling angel directly behind it. Nowhere in Scripture is this even remotely suggested. But as a part of his world plan, Satan will try to gain control of organisational bodies, whether that means industry, the media, political structures or even the church (or maybe I should say, especially the church). Demonic control will be exerted through areas of vulnerability. For example, a business structure looking for a healthy profit margin will be susceptible to the demonic control of finance. A church, proud of its fine tradition of music and worship, will run the risk of concentrating its efforts on building up and maintaining that tradition, at the expense of its obedience to God. Where Satan gains a hold in this way, that hold has to be broken, and that can only happen by real repentance of the initial wrong exercise of choice, and submission to God.

All of us, individuals and institutions alike, are most vulnerable in our main areas of calling. Just suppose, for example, that we have a real gift for charity work and organisation. It is all too easy to take on all sorts of responsibilities just because it panders to our ego. To put it another way, it makes us feel good to be 'helping'. But God might actually have very different plans for us, which we just will not respond to because we like what we are doing. That is rebellion, and the devil is delighted—even if it appears that we are doing all sorts of good.

Or suppose we are that self-same big charity, and we see a way of 'doing good' that is entirely in line with our charitable purposes . . . but it involves bending the law a little, or doing something of which we are not very proud. If we go down that road it opens up the way for the devil to get a hold. He gets a handle over us, which will grow stronger over time. Unless it is broken. It will always remain and give rise to problems, unless and until it is repented of and broken.

Not only that. Where a demonic hold grows in strength, and gets a real grip over an organisation or structure, it will become actively hostile to anything that challenges its power. This hold need not be obviously bad. The devil is quite capable of dangling some attractive titbits before our noses. We may, for example, belong to a large corporate organisation whose business ventures go to underpin the economic structure of the society in which we live. Or we may belong to the academic staff of a major university, renowned throughout the world for its leading position in scholarship. The structures of such organisations may very well have become corroded. If it should then happen that the ruling spirit is challenged, maybe by an employee who is all too obviously out of step with the governing ethos, then the ruling spirit may well become hostile to that individual and, if it does not succeed in ousting the individual from the organisation, may well try and discredit and limit his or her influence.

Conclusion

Scripture consistently shows us that angels are used by God for the government and implementation of his purposes in the world. It attests to different orders of angels (eg, Colossians 1:15–16; Romans 8:38–39) and it implies angelic oversight of individual nations and cities (Daniel 12). We may not see these spiritual beings—in fact we most probably shall not—but that is no reason to discount their existence and activity. Just as there are good angels serving the purposes of the Lord (some of which purposes may well include punishment and destruction: eg, Genesis 19:1-29), so too there are fallen angels, whose activities are determined by their hostility to God. The latter, however, are still under the sovereignty of God, and God has set limits to the extent of their activities. Where they want to go beyond these limits, they have to seek permission (as we see, for example, in Satan's request to 'sift' Peter, countered by Jesus' own intervention: Luke 22:31-32). While permission may sometimes be granted for attack (and indeed God will at times permit all of us to be exposed to this, and even maybe on occasion fall before it, in order that we might come to know him better and grow in our faith), our safety and victory are absolutely assured by our obedience. In every aspect of our lives we should mirror the sovereignty and honour of God.

So often, even those of us who are Christians bemoan the terrible things that happen to us, oblivious to the fact that certain areas of our lives are tainted by the 'worship of other gods'. Obedience and submission actually ensure protection; disobedience may mean withdrawal of that protection. Conversely, where God has a purpose for us (as he did with the Children of Israel and, of course, with Jesus himself), he may well allow us to be exposed to the most terrible attack in order that we might be trained. At the end of the day, at one level it is the same thing that is going on: the exposing of sin or inadequate understanding in order that we might be purified and strengthened. But at another level the process is radically different. People often say that it is the 'good' who seem to suffer most. Sadly, this is often true, because Satan targets God's children who love him, and if he cannot deceive them into wrongdoing, he tries to wear them down and disable them by attack.

The devil attacks us wherever we are vulnerable. Unsubmitted areas are vulnerable. At the same time, God trains his children for battle. He has to if he wants us to serve him and to use us, especially for the winning of others. If he did not train us, we would get blown away by our first encounter with evil; so he gives us combat training. This means that he will sometimes give Satan permission to attack us (as we have already seen in Chapter 3 on temptation), in order that we might see what we are up against and, most importantly of all, that we might see God's power in operation, and so stand. In the army, soldiers have to learn discipline and undergo training before they are allowed into combat. If this did not happen, they would be annihilated. It is the same for us, and the greater the call, the more comprehensive and extensive the training has to be. We have to learn discipline, and we have to learn to use God's power in the right way. Seen or unseen, angels and demons are a part of this whole process.

11
Curses

The devil would like to fool us into believing he has the monopoly on curses. Use that word today, in fact, and for a lot of people it will stir up images of the Evil Eye and witches' covens ... the stuff of which horror movies are made! And precisely because of those connotations, others dismiss the whole idea out of hand. To many modern men and women—nurtured as we have been on a diet of strict scientific rationalism—the idea that some kind of malign and evil power could possibly be exerting any type of hold seems both archaic and ludicrous.

The Bible, however, presents a rather different picture, and we need to understand this if we are to get any kind of real perception of what is going on, and if we are going to avoid the errors of either kind of extreme. In this chapter, we shall distinguish between two very different types of curse. First, the curses that are the product of God's wrath, and that are the divine response to sin. And, second, curses produced by the deliberate focusing of a malign and hostile spiritual influence. As precursor to this, however, we need first to understand the interrelationship between the spiritual and material worlds.

Background

We live in a materialistic age. That fact is so self-evident that for many in the West at least it goes without saying. This, however, goes far beyond a simple commitment to consumerism. What it means is that all of us tend to live life solely at its manifest level. We assume that what goes on in the visible world is the sole level of reality, and that what we achieve is directly related to the level of physical effort we have put in to the task in hand. The more we do, the more successful we shall be. This, however, is not the biblical understanding of life.

The Bible teaches that men and women are made up of body, mind and spirit, or, to put it another way, we are spiritual beings who have a physical body. What this means is that there is a whole spiritual world of which we are a part, and that what is seen is not the whole story. But the Bible does not stop there. It stresses that the spiritual and the physical are not just inextricably linked, but one underlies the other, and whatever takes place at a spiritual level will have repercussions physically. We see this, for example, in and through the Fall. Adam and Eve rupture their relationship with God through disobedience, and the physical result is that they are no longer permitted (nor even able) to live in the Garden of Eden. The loss of their close relationship with God has affected the way in which they are able to live their lives from that point on, and even though they might want to, they can never by themselves get back to Eden—because cherubim now bar the way (Genesis 3:24)!

Similarly, in Zechariah 3, in the confrontation between the angel of the Lord and Satan, as the two dispute for possession of the high priest Joshua, it is clear that the fate of Jerusalem is actually at stake, and that this is an argument in the heavenly places that will have repercussions within the material world.

The Bible in fact consistently teaches that what happens at the material or natural level is an outworking and reflection of the spiritual. However, not only does what happen in the heavenly places have a direct bearing on what takes place in the natural world, but the quality of the individual's relationship with God directly affects his or her earthly life. Furthermore, the Bible teaches that in order to achieve things at a natural level, whether military success, prosperity or even good health, the first thing to get right is the relationship with God. Everything, in fact, depends on that. On every page of the Bible we find the underlying belief that visible success in life, prosperity—and even good health—depend on the spiritual.

This is not to say that those who stand in close relationship with God have no problems and are unbelievably rich. This is quite patently not the case, whether we are talking of such giants as Elijah and Paul or even Jesus himself . . . or, at the other end of the spectrum, people as humble as Priscilla and Aquila, co-workers with the Apostle Paul, who were expelled from Rome simply because they happened to be Jews (Acts 18:1–2). Close relationship with God can actually attract its own problems, but that is a different issue. What we are talking about here is the clear and unshakable belief, fundamental to both Jewish and Christian doctrine, that if the spiritual base is lacking, deficient, or otherwise impaired (that is, if our relationship with God is not right) then, whatever preparations are made, ultimately they will either fail completely or the result will be badly flawed.

If we want to see this in the Bible, then we have only to look at the fortunes of Israel. Time and again they were threatened by the hostile nations that stood round about. When they were obedient to Yahweh's commands and put their trust in him, then even if they did nothing at all, their enemies were put to confusion and routed (eg, 1 Kings 20:28). But if they disobeyed (and especially if they worshipped foreign gods), absolute disaster followed, whether it was plague and sickness, military defeat, or even simply social breakdown (compare, for example, the picture presented in Amos 1–4).

What many people do not like to acknowledge in our Western, effort-centred culture is that what was true for Israel is just as true for us today: get right with God, and everything else falls into place. Again, it must be emphasised that this is not to put forward the so-called 'prosperity gospel'. To be in close relationship with God does not mean that we will never encounter problems ever again, nor does it mean that we shall all become millionaires overnight. But it does mean that ultimately everything will work for our good, because God himself will fight for us and defend us, and we shall have real joy because of that—and not many people in the West today have actually experienced joy! When we are right with God, then even the difficult and painful times are not just okay, but actually in time even become tremendous blessing . . . which brings us specifically to the questions: What are blessings and curses, and how do they operate?

Divine response to sin

To put it simply, blessings and curses are vehicles of spiritual power. In the Bible, the base line is that blessing is God's response to obedience; it is the release and outpouring of God's power *for good*, activated by that obedience. A curse, on the other hand, is the activation of his wrath in response to disobedience.

As early as Exodus, Yahweh tells his people that this is how he is going to respond to them; it is a part of the covenant relationship he has entered into with them. We must be clear at this point that the activation of curse is not judgement or rejection, but is actually a part of God's love, because it is only in this way that he can teach his chosen people when they go astray and ultimately keep them faithful to him. It is from this covenant relationship then that we can understand how seriously God views sin or turning away from him. God tells his people, not just that he is going to respond to them in this way, but that where they wilfully turn from him and follow after other gods, his wrath will carry on down to the third and fourth generations. Now this is very serious, because not only does it mean that God reacts to what we do and think, and this has a tangible effect in our lives, but that what we do will also have an effect on our children and grandchildren, and so on down the generations. God states this explicitly in the Ten Commandments:

> You shall not make for yourself an idol in the form of anything in heaven above or on the earth beneath or in the waters below. You shall not bow down to them or worship them; for I, the Lord your God, am a jealous God, punishing the children for the sin of the fathers to the third and fourth generation of those who hate me, but showing love to a thousand generations of those who love me and keep my commandments (Exodus 20:4–6).

Blessings and curses are an integral part of the covenant relationship. It is almost as if God is saying, 'I'm sorry, but that's the way I am! You know me now, so you have a choice. Where there is disobedience and turning away, then my wrath is going to be provoked, because that's the way I respond to sin. But if you keep faith with me, it's going to be great!'

Again, in Deuteronomy 28 we find clearly spelled out the blessings for obedience and curses for disobedience, and it is a chapter that makes incredible reading. Specifically, where the people turn from him and disobey, we find the dire warning: 'The Lord will send on you curses, confusion and rebuke in everything you put your hand to, until you are destroyed and come to sudden ruin because of the evil you have done in forsaking him' (Deuteronomy 28:20). The list that follows is extremely comprehensive, but the truly awe-inspiring thing is to see how these words subsequently take effect. Like it or not, their force is not confined exclusively to the Old Testament.

Our worldview today is such that we tend to dismiss the plain meaning of these words as unbelievably archaic. We automatically assume that they cannot possibly be true, because God simply cannot be like that. After all, we reassure ourselves, 'God is love', and this is plain nasty! Actually, sin matters precisely because God is love.

God is such that he will not compromise with sin—and he will not compromise with sin in our lives, because sin is the barrier that separates us from himself. That is why the devil tries to tempt us to sin, because each time we fall we take a step away from God, and if God did not do something, we would never be able to get back to him and be freed! Today we often find it very difficult to understand that God meant what he said in the Ten Commandments, but we ought to realise just how serious he was—and is—because of what happened to Jesus. God could not waive the penalty for sin because it was too important. So, to save us from being destroyed, *he made his own Son a curse*. As Paul puts it in Galatians, 'Christ redeemed us from the curse of the law by becoming a curse for us . . .' (3:13).

In this context, then, a curse is the penalty for transgression of God's law. It has nothing to do with Satan in the first instance, and everything to do with God's flouted love. On the cross Christ broke the hold of Satan over our lives, true, but he also cleared us of the deserved penalty of God's wrath, by taking in his own person our sins. Without that divine penalty, Satan cannot get at us, because he only has legitimate access through sin (for anything beyond that he has to have permission).

On the cross, then, *we* are crucified with Christ—our sin is crucified—which means that from that point on we live in Christ's life, washed with his righteousness. The devil has no hold over Jesus, because Jesus never sinned—so that means that when we are wearing Christ's righteousness, he has nothing against us! But this does not happen automatically, despite what some people maintain. For Christ to take away our sin, that sin has to be repented of. Unrepented sin means that we are still under God's wrath . . . which is very silly, because God does not want us to be under his wrath. Where there is unrepented sin, the devil can and will gain access, and he will assert a claim through, and because of, that sin. Where someone is experiencing tremendous problems, it may be that there is a curse in place because of disobedience. Where that is the case it needs repentance, and a coming before God in humility to ask for release. Focusing on the devil here in rebuke is not very helpful, because in a perverted kind of way it is still actually giving worship to 'false gods' rather than to God himself. It is God who needs to be at the centre.

Now, as we have seen, that curse may not be in response to anything we have done ourselves. It may be in response to something done by our ancestors generations back. Where this is the case, the same principle holds good. Unless and until the specific area of sin, where the hold was first established, is repented of and renounced, and sealed by Christ's blood, it will be like a bleeding wound in our side, spoiling our lives—our relationships, our work, our emotional well-being. Christ, by his death, has broken the curse of God's wrath . . . but we have to allow him to do that. Otherwise, if we turn a blind eye to a specific area of sin in our lives, or in the lives of our ancestors, the devil says, 'They never repented of this. They invited me in here . . . I'm staying. This is my territory!'

Having said that, however, a word of much needed caution! We should not get hung up on the devil here, nor should we go searching after sin. Rather, we need to trust God. True, there are certain things that we must most definitely repent of when we come into a real relationship with God—things such as past occult involvement, dabbling with ouija boards when children, sexual sin . . . and of course, things like cherished hurt, anger and bitterness. But the problem is, the list can seem dauntingly long when we look at some of the books around, and if we are not careful we can actually very soon feel we are so awful that God cannot possibly love us and never will . . . as much as anything else, because we simply cannot remember every sin. Not true. God does love us, and he knows how pathetic we are. What God actually requires of us is simply a willingness to let him in . . . and he will do the rest. We can trust him one hundred per cent to look after us. Whether it is our own sin, or generational sin committed by our ancestors way back, we can have absolute trust in God that he will bring that knowledge to us as and when necessary.

Let me try to explain what I mean. When we first come to know Christ, he sends the Holy Spirit to begin to sort us out and he makes a promise to us that he will heal and cleanse us of all the imperfections of our lives and that he will, one day, get us back to our heavenly home. To use the theological jargon popularised by St Augustine, from the minute we come to know Christ, we are saved, and from then on he works on our full redemption. It is as a part of this progressive healing that God, over time, shows us areas of our lives that are displeasing to him, or to which we have (perhaps unknowingly) denied him access. He will do this as and when we are ready to respond, and only when the time is right. He will not show us everything in one fell swoop when we first get to know him, because if he did that we would just be blown apart; but he will lead us very gently, and reveal different things at different times. His way of revealing things can actually at the time involve quite a bit of discomfort. We may find that things on which we have relied are suddenly (and none too gently) taken from us; we may feel that everything just piles up and we can no longer cope; we may become ill; we may find ourselves suddenly subjected to a form of temptation that we thought we had long gone beyond.

I have had so many people of deep faith coming to me with such a huge range of problems, and so quick to blame the devil, when actually all that was happening was that the Lord was wanting to touch a specific area of their lives—and wanting to touch them for blessing. The Lord will do this with every one of us, simply because we are all so flawed. But we do not need to look for the problems. Provided we have repented of all that we consciously know to be wrong, God will show us any problem areas in his own good time—but he will only reveal them to us as and when we are ready for them to be dealt with. We should not therefore be afraid when these seemingly insoluble problems arise, no matter what they are. It may be that we have no idea why things persistently seem to go wrong. In that situation we should simply ask the Lord to show us the cause, with fasting if need be, and not be deterred until he does. In all things we need simply to remember that God is sovereign, and then be obedient to his leading.

Of course, there are different scenarios. Where we deliberately sin, then the Lord will respond in wrath in order to bring us to that point of repentance and back to himself. At the same time, where sin is deliberate, the devil will have straight access into our lives at that point, because succumbing is like a gilt-edged invitation card! But where we are caught (or even just titillated) by sin in this way, I do not believe that the troubles which often seem to arise are caused by the devil at all—I think he would actually like everything to go very well, so that we become further caught in his net. I believe that God often 'withdraws' his protection, just as he did with the Israelites, so that things go 'naturally' wrong (maybe because of some of those past 'hidden' personal or generational sins). We are allowed to experience the consequences of our own acts, especially of our disobedience. Again, this kind of situation needs repentance. If there is no repentance, then not only shall we suffer the consequences of those sinful acts but, as we have already seen spelled out in the Bible, our children and the generations to come shall also suffer the consequences. Yet remember, God's aim is always to bring us back to himself.

Where we sin, but at the same time in other areas of our lives turn actively to God, then not only will God be working to restore us, but at this point, I believe, the devil will become overtly hostile and begin to attack. Difficulties and misfortunes that are the result of such attack have the aim of destruction, and require rebuke. Again, however, the first thing needed is a real turning back to God in repentance (and asking him, if need be, what it is we need to be repenting of). Then, and only then, after we have repented, can we begin to resist and rebuke the devil with success.

In the spiritual realm the devil can see very clearly what God is doing. He can see both where God is performing a work of salvation in someone's life, and also where he is preparing them for some task ahead. Both of these things he will try to prevent. Now the New Testament tells us very clearly, 'Resist the devil, and he will flee from you' (James 4:7). But the beginning of this verse is instructive and in things written on spiritual warfare it is frequently overlooked: 'Submit yourselves, then, to God.' We resist the devil and break his hold by first submitting ourselves to God, and by thanking and praising him for all he has done.

Let me try to illustrate what I mean by all of this. I freqently say that if I were to park on double yellow lines, then even if there were a dozen other cars parked there and no one taking the slightest notice of them, I would be the one to get a ticket. And this really does seem to be true. I can do something 'slightly' wrong like this, that other people seem to do without a second thought, and immediately I get caught. I have stopped doing anything like this, in fact—not because I am incredibly honest, but because I know the consequences! If I do something wrong, I get found out. I believe that God is actually trying to teach me something important about truth and purity—and that he is not going to let up on me until I have learned (at which point of course it will no longer be necessary!).

The second situation, where the attack is straight from the devil, is rather different, and requires first and foremost a 'listening to God' in order to deal with it. The answer may be surprising! This is perhaps rather harder to illustrate, but here is an example: about nine months ago our son became very ill. My first reaction was panic, but I felt God telling me not to panic, but instead to be still with him. The trouble was, our son did not seem to be getting any better, so I began to ask God if there was some sin on our part that was causing this. Interestingly, in prayer, others felt it was things said against us by others that was the cause . . . and then I felt God whispering to me that I had not always perhaps been quite as enthusiastic as I might have been about his calling for my life in *my* comments! But none of this actually seemed to be the whole cause behind what was happening, and our son did not get miraculously better. And then—after an enormous amount of prayer—I felt God saying that we were being attacked because we were doing his work, and that he had been attacked while on earth too; but not to worry, because he had conquered.

Sounds easy, doesn't it? At this point I began sternly to rebuke the devil, but I felt God telling me to be quiet. Instead, I felt him telling me again to praise, and have peace, and he would deal with it, because it was *his* battle. And he gave me tremendous assurance that it was and would be all right. As I write this, our son is slowly recovering, and we pray that he will be healed totally, but we have learned some important lessons both about the devil's hostility and God's power through all of this. So I would say to people now, even if you are in the middle of what feels to be a very severe attack, go very gently into 'warfare'. Submit first to God and be led by him. Listen to him and obey whatever he says.

Contrary to much popular opinion, I do not believe there are always ready answers to suffering and difficulty in life. There are no formulae of cause and effect—and people can cause tremendous harm when they try rigidly to apply these formulae to the lives of others. However, there is a complete answer in our relationship with God, and it is this, above all else, that we all need to work at. The important thing is to be in the kind of relationship with God where we can hear what it is he is saying to us—and then to listen and be obedient.

The curse of generational sin

Sometimes, where there is a real ancestral curse going back over generations, then it may actually take a while for that to be broken, and freedom from that only becomes real when the individual has learned what it means to stand in Christ. I have in mind the kind of scenario where there has been a family history of repeated marital breakdown, and maybe alcohol abuse and even suicide. For example, someone already in an unhappy marriage comes and asks for prayer, in the course of which an ancestral curse is quite clearly broken. It is my experience that although something has fundamentally changed, there are still mopping-up operations needed with the different situations of that person's life, and what one actually sees from that moment on is a real growth of relationship with God, that gently over time leads to a total transformation of life . . . and real joy. However, while not discounting the possibility, I have not yet encountered the situation where everything has suddenly become totally all right overnight. This is not to say that it is God's will that this happens. But in this situation, I think the devil has capitalised on God's response to sin, using weapons such as guilt, fear, self-loathing and the like, and it takes a while fully to appropriate the freedom given by God. I believe God sometimes permits this kind of 'prolonged healing' in order that the individual might fully realise the gift and power of his love.

Blessing

A lot has been said about curses here, but something more needs to be said about blessing. Blessing, as we have seen, is God's response to obedience. It is the outpouring of his love for good. Incredible as it may seem, God actually wants us to live in and enjoy this good always. He wants to bless us, but a lot of things can get in the way of our receiving all that he wants to give us, and one of the biggest obstacles is sometimes ourselves.

We block God's blessing for a whole host of reasons—for example, anxiety, guilt, fear, anger, pain. The reverse side of the coin of blessing is our thankfulness and praise. This is why, in fact, praise is such an important weapon in spiritual warfare—it opens us up and allows us to focus on God, so that he can then pour into us his blessing. And it is as we get right with him spiritually that his power is poured out at a material level—and order and well-being start to emerge out of our chaos.

But we find too, in the Bible, that not just words but objects can become vehicles for blessing; that is, for the release of God's power. Most clearly, in the Old Testament, we see this in the oil of blessing. When someone was appointed by God for a specific task, he was then anointed with oil. Samuel, for example, anointed first Saul and then David as king over Israel. The underlying idea was that God had chosen these men to rule over his people, but his power was released in them for the task only by and through the anointing with oil, which released in them his Spirit. Thus Saul, immediately following on his anointing, was filled with the Spirit of God and, for the first time in his life, started to prophesy (1 Samuel 10:9–13). The blessing given by Samuel had, therefore, released in Saul the power of God—but, importantly, it was only by this power that Saul was enabled to fulfil the task to which he had been appointed. Here, then, the oil of blessing was the vehicle for God's *enabling* power.

In the New Testament we find the same idea most powerfully in the bread and the wine taken and blessed by Jesus at the Last Supper. Jesus said to the disciples,

'This is my body,' and a little later, 'This is my blood.' But there was something far more powerful than simply symbol at work here. In his first letter to the Corinthian church, Paul wrote: 'Is not the cup of thanksgiving for which we give thanks a participation in the blood of Christ? And is not the bread that we break a participation in the body of Christ?' (1 Corinthians 10:16).

So here, once the bread and the wine had been blessed, they became vehicles for the release of God's blessing to believers. This is not to imply that they had in some way become magically transformed, but the power of God for blessing was at work in them. Equally, if anyone then participated in the communion in an unworthy manner (that is, in a state of conscious sin) then they ate judgement on themselves—because at that point God's wrath would be activated by disobedience:

> Whoever eats the bread or drinks the cup of the Lord in an unworthy manner will be guilty of sinning against the body and blood of the Lord. A man ought to examine himself before he eats of the bread and drinks of the cup. For anyone who eats and drinks without recognising the body of the Lord eats and drinks judgement on himself. That is why many among you are weak and sick, and a number of you have fallen asleep. But if we judged ourselves, we would not come under judgement. When we are judged by the Lord, we are being disciplined so that we will not be condemned with the world (1 Corinthians 11:27–32).

The deliberate focusing of a malign and hostile force

In Numbers 22 we have the strange story of Balak, king of Moab, summoning Balaam to curse the Israelites:

'Now come and put a curse on these people, because they are too powerful for me. Perhaps then I will be able to defeat them and drive them out of the country. For I know that those you bless are blessed, and those you curse are cursed' (Numbers 22:6).

What followed, however, is even more strange, because Yahweh apparently took the potential threat so seriously that he sent an angel to impede the seer's journey. Balaam's curse was obviously so potent that it threatened the whole future of Israel and, because of this, God would not allow it to be pronounced, because his will was for blessing, and not harm.

Now this is interesting, because it reflects the Hebrew idea that a spoken curse was an active agent for hurt. Yet this in itself was only a part of their far wider belief in the creative and dynamic force inherent in words because, in common with the peoples among whom they lived, the Israelites believed that spiritual power became creatively manifest through outgoing words. For example, they believed that God brought all of creation into being by the sending out of his word (see Genesis 1:2ff.; John 1:1f.). But they did not just believe that this was a one-off occurrence—the verbal equivalent to the Big Bang. They believed, as ongoing reality, that once God's word had gone out, it would take effect, and it was this that gave such force to prophecy. To the Israelites, therefore, prophetic utterance was seen as powerful—not just because it was a foretelling of the future, but because it was the forth-speaking (in the sense of *out*speaking) of God's word, and the act of giving it utterance brought it into being. Behind the word, therefore, was the Spirit of God, which held dynamic power for both blessing and curse. It could not return to him empty, and for this reason the prophets were felt to wield tremendous power.

Balaam was just such a 'man of God', the ancient name for a prophet. Although there is no suggestion that he was a prophet of Yahweh, he was clearly seen as spiritually powerful, so that the words he spoke held creative power, whether for good or ill.

A curse, then, is the utterance of words to bring about destruction, and depends for effect upon the spiritual power that lies behind the utterance. Through a curse, the Israelites believed, an active agent for harm is sent forth. That God himself took this seriously in this rather bizarre but appealing story in Numbers, indicates that there is something we need to take seriously too.

There is undeniably a power in words, as indeed attested to in the New Testament by James: '. . . no man can tame the tongue. It is a restless evil, full of deadly poison' (3:8). All of us, I am sure, can dredge from our memories remarks made to us in the past that have had a powerful effect on the whole of the rest of our lives. Sometimes these comments work for good, but other times they can have a cripplingly devastating effect.

Someone came to see me recently who as a child had not only been badly rejected by her mother, but had been constantly told that she was evil. The result of all this anger, pain and fear was not only a breakdown in her twenties, but a total inability to relate to people in a normal way. She was constantly afraid people were going to find out 'the truth' about her, and discover how bad she really was. This poor lady really was iron-bound by things that had been said to her, and needed to be freed to discover how nice she was, so that she could enjoy life!

Things we say to ourselves can also have this effect. But interestingly, too, while we may not be specifically making internal vows that can damage us, a constant focusing on problems and the negative aspects of our lives can also reinforce these things and lead us away from God.

This may sound a little odd, but just suppose someone has said something about us that is extremely derogatory and puts us in a bad light, but which actually has no foundation in fact. They have said this behind our backs, and somehow it reaches our ears. Now rationally we know that we should dismiss it. It is untrue, so we can consign it to the Lord. But our brain takes a rather different route. We begin to feel really worried that this has been said about us. We worry about the effect it is going to have on others who will hear about it—and maybe justifiably, because we live in a world where sadly we do all like to believe the worst about others. So we worry that maybe these comments are going to damage us—but we do not know how to counter them, because they have not been made directly to us, nor do we know how many people they have been passed on to. So we start to worry. It nags at the back of our mind, making us edgy and quick tempered. Then it seems to take over our mind—anger and anxiety almost equally mixed. And then something very strange happens—we begin to wonder if maybe the comments are true. Maybe we really are like that, only we have not realised. On top of all that anxiety, we begin to doubt ourselves. And suddenly, everywhere we look, all we can see is the terrible effect of these words.

A focusing on the negative intensifies the negative. It is a part of the deception practised by Satan in the battle for our minds, and unless we consciously turn away, it can have a devastating effect. It is very powerfully here that praise actually cracks open the mould and allows God's power to flood through. It is coming against the spiritual power attacking us in the opposing spirit. And, believe me, it works. Never be disabled by the thought, 'This has absolutely nothing to do with spiritual things at all. This is a real problem.' Yes, it is a real problem, but that reality is only a manifestation of the spiritual forces at work; and, if we give in to them, we get sucked in. So don't. Look away—recognise it for what it is, and resist. Focus on God, and let him deal with the problem.

Now at the same time, people can quite definitely harm us by criticisms and expressed hostility (whether made directly to us or not) and this harm is not just a projection of our imagination; it is real. As we see from the Balaam story, it is the spiritual force behind the words that becomes operative and that in turn becomes an active agent for harm. We should be very careful with words because they can cause great harm, and can all too easily become a vehicle for the devil to use. It is often said that a curse cannot come to rest without cause, and that is true, but none of us in this life is wholly without sin. We can both cause and receive harm by ill-considered words. If for no other reason than our own spiritual health, we should keep a guard on our tongues.

It sometimes also happens these days that people caught up in popularist folk magic ideas will actively try to conjure up harm against someone else. Sometimes this is done jokingly; but occasionally it is in deadly earnest. It cannot be stressed too strongly how dangerous this is, not least for the people involved. They are dabbling with things that are enormously powerful spiritually, and they lay themselves open to tremendous harm.

Around Oxfordshire we not only regularly have psychic fairs taking place, with a lot of very odd practices involved, but there are also quite a large number of active covens, which are openly hostile to Christianity. I believe we should take seriously the idea of curses placed upon us as Christians, because such active intentions for harm can cause terrible damage, especially if we are weak in the Lord. But I also believe in the absolute sovereignty of God. These spirits are already defeated and have to give place before the Lord.

It is the curse of the Lord that we should truly fear. Satan is a defeated foe and he knows it, along with all his demonic hordes. This does not mean that we should take him lightly. He remains a fallen angel of immense spiritual power and we are a part of fallen humanity. But in Christ we are anointed with the power of God and, in obedience, we share in victory. Our obedience activates the blessing of protection.

12
The Devil Today

> He [Satan] was a murderer from the beginning, not holding to the truth, for there is no truth in him. When he lies, he speaks his native language, for he is a liar and the father of lies (John 8:44).

Not for nothing did Jesus call Satan a murderer and the father of lies. That, in a nutshell, is his character and primary aim in relation to men and women even today: deception and destruction. Though he will do all in his power to lead us away from God and focus the worship we should rightfully give to God on himself, at no point is his will towards us ever good. The underlying aim of his ensnarement is in fact destruction—and his ultimate triumph is when we actually destroy ourselves. We need to understand this, especially in view of the fact that so much temptation is to apparent good.

As we have already seen, the devil (in his essential being) is not creative and, because of this, is inferior to God. He is simply not capable of going off and calling into being his own world and so, no matter how much he may dislike it, he remains under God's sovereignty. Nevertheless, he is a powerful spiritual being and his will is to usurp God's position.

The illustration I always like is that of the bridgehead being established in France in the Second World War after the D-Day landings. The decisive battle, military analysts tell us, had been fought, and the total removal of the enemy was assured, but it was still necessary for the Allies to sweep through the country, dealing with pockets of resistance and wiping out all traces of enemy occupation. This is the situation we are in today. Satan has been defeated, but enemy forces are still infesting the land (even though they know they are fighting a rearguard action). Now they have to be dealt with in order for men and women really to experience the freedom Christ has brought. In Mark 13:10ff. Jesus told the disciples that only when every nation had had the opportunity to respond to the gospel would God move to wipe out totally every trace of Satan's evil presence and effect.

But for this time, although his influence is extensive, Satan's weapons are actually only suggestion and deception. More than anything else, he loves to try and twist the truth. Beyond this, unless given express permission by God, he has no power . . . unless and until, that is, we give him and his minions permission to work through us. What this means in practical terms is that we can and will be tempted—just as Jesus himself was—but Satan will have no actual power over and through us until we succumb. Having said this, however, it is not always easy to recognise when we are being tempted, and there will be occasions when, without God, we most certainly fall. Some temptations, it must be said, can appear both desirable and good. Some can even appear to hold the best interests of others at their heart . . . and some can appear as words of God!

To give a very straightforward example of what I

mean by this, I find that there is always a temptation to respond to requests by people for ministry and prayer. It is indeed all too easy to get snowed under by such requests, and then to justify any ensuing problems, family rows or general fatigue, by the fact that God wanted me to help. I have had to learn, often painfully, that this is very far from the truth and that I must respond to others only at God's direction. Along the way, I have then identified a number of temptations.

First, it is all too easy to believe that only *we* can help. This is both powerful and subtle, but actually we never help; we can only be channels for God. When we become blocked by this kind of temptation, our effectiveness is severely impaired—because there is too much 'us' and not enough God! Second, there is a particularly compelling temptation to martyrdom, which may sound a little odd, but let me explain. Such ministry is very tiring. I find there are definite limits which I must not go beyond, or I can come near to physical collapse myself, and will most certainly fall prey to every passing cold or flu bug there is. Having said that, however, it is still very easy to go beyond those limits, and then to feel a kind of self-righteous satisfaction, 'Poor little me. I am feeling so weary and have this terrible cold because I have done so much good!' What a joke! But God has had quite a difficult time teaching me that he requires my obedience, and not my collapse. Third, and most important of course, there is the temptation to become so busy that God is pushed out of the picture entirely. As so many people in ministry will testify, when they are *very* busy, then one of the first things to go or be cut back on, is the time spent alone with God. When this happens we become spiritually weak and, yet again, ineffective.

First and foremost, then, we should not underestimate the power or subtlety of temptation, and our primary aim should be to come closer to God in order that we might recognise it for what it is. Second, we need to be aware that where Satan has gained a foothold, then (to continue the military analogy) politely asking him to go will have very little effect. Where a country is in the process of liberation from hostile occupying forces, simply walking into a town square and saying, 'I say, chaps, would you mind coming out now with your hands up and then leaving?' will probably only achieve one result: you get shot. The devil is not well-mannered and, even though in defeat, he is not prepared to give ground without a struggle. So for our part we have to be determined, well-trained and well-armed, and we also have to be absolutely obedient to our Commander-in-chief.

We also need to work together with others, because a battalion working under one single command is far more effective than a solitary sniper, no matter how effective a shot he is. The devil, however, knows this just as much as we do and it disturbs him. One of his major lines of defence, therefore, is to sow confusion among the troops and, when not totally submitted to God, we very easily fall prey to this method of attack. It is in fact wholly remarkable how much suspicion, mistrust and downright dislike there is among Christians—and we, more than any others, are the people who are supposed to love each other! So let us look first at how the devil attempts to achieve some of these ends.

Forms of temptation

Perversion of truth

The devil's classic line of attack is not to implant in the mind some totally off-the-wall suggestion that any right thinking person would immediately reject. Rather, it is to work from a central kernel of truth, very subtly distorted so that it leads the mind into a totally wrong perception. For example, I share the biblical view that to follow pagan religions and cults is, in some sense, to give worship to the devil/demons. Now, contrary to what many people assume if you say this, it does not mean that you automatically condemn all adherents of other religions as evil: in some sense deluded, yes—but evil, no. What it does mean is that there are, woven into these beliefs, some very real and precious God-given truths, but they have been distorted in such a way as to lead away from God, and focus the individual on things that actually reinforce that existential state of separation so vividly described in the narrative of the Fall.

If you look, for example, at so many of the meditation-based techniques that are around today. All without exception claim to lead the individual effortlessly to self-fulfilment or 'realisation'. Now at one level the aims contained within these teachings are entirely right, because what God wants for each one of us is that we should find our total fulfilment, and be freed in every sense from the damaging effects of sin. But in fact it is a myth that we can find this kind of release anywhere apart from God, because only God is capable of setting us free from sin. Let me try and explain a little what I mean.

It is remarkable how all modern teachings, no matter how much they hold out the goal of fulfilment, wipe away the idea of sin. Many New Age ideas will admit of right and wrong action, but by this they mean those things that support the fulfilment of the individual, as opposed to those things that in some way impose a constraint. Ideas of right and wrong are therefore wholly relative. That is, what is right for me might well be wrong for you, but there is no objective truth. (Indeed, what is right for me at any one time may well be wrong for me in two weeks' time, so even for the individual there is no objective standard by which to live.) They deny that there is any good, as absolute, by which we ought to live, in the process apparently oblivious of the fact that their denial of 'absolute' is in itself the affirmation of an alternative absolute.

Well and good, you might think. If they want to think that, fine! Who's to say we are right? But this leads us to a very real problem, which is not simply unanswered, but wholly untouched by this kind of view. Problem: one may say there is no objective wrong, but no one in his right mind could possibly say that the motiveless slaughter of millions (as happened with the Holocaust) was right. And if, perversely, someone did try to maintain this on the ground that the individuals responsible needed to pursue this course of action for their own particular fulfilment, then let him consider how he would respond if someone tried to murder, or sexually interfere with, his child. To counter this kind of argument with the response, 'Ah yes, but here we have a situation where their good is in conflict with mine,' is absurd, because how could such a detrimental invasion of another possibly constitute a 'good', no matter what kind of a high it gave the perpetrator?

Any right thinking person, therefore, has to admit that there is such a thing as right and wrong as objective reality and, once that is admitted, then logically they have to admit the existence of sin. But New Age teachings reject the idea of sin! They start with a basic truth—that the goal of every individual is release into self-fulfilment—but this has been twisted in such a way as to make that release impossible, because it places the emphasis on the individual to obtain that release (although by-passing the concept of sinful wrongdoing), and thereby totally removes the possibility of divine forgiveness and restoration.

If we pause to think for a minute we can immediately see the practical implications of this way of thinking, and at every level of life. Anyone who has ever felt the slightest shred of emotion or talked with another human being will know the crippling effects of guilt and the very real human need that there is for forgiveness (operating of course both ways). A lady came to see me some time ago suffering from panic attacks. In the course of conversation she admitted that some years previously she had been involved in an adulterous relationship. It was only in confessing to God and experiencing forgiveness that she was healed. It would have been simply no good to have said to this lady, 'Never mind. What you did wasn't wrong, it was simply what you needed at the time.' She had been trying to say that to herself for years and it had not worked. But in coming to Christ she was healed.

The plain fact is that all of us, where there is wrong in our lives, need to receive God's forgiveness—whether we know it or not—because without that we remain bound by sin and therefore tied to death. But not only do contrary teachings prevent the individual from receiving the healing and freedom that he or she needs and that *only* God can give—but, strange as it may sound, they can also themselves become a form of bondage. In the course of ministry I have come across many individuals who have felt themselves 'caught' by these teachings—not just in the sense of some sort of psychological predisposition, but in ways that have actually crippled their lives.

This was very clearly illustrated to me by another lady I came across who was profoundly influenced by the I Ching (a very ancient Chinese astrological system). Far from leading to freedom, the book set up a very real kind of spiritual hold, because she would not do anything without consulting it and, if the forecast was bad, that was it! But this lady also complained of a feeling of spiritual forces around her. The effect was only broken when she repented of her involvement and the book was destroyed.

We are talking of pseudo-religious teachings and their effects here, of course, but it must be pointed out that the devil does not limit his field of operations solely to religion. Wherever he attacks, the same principle holds good. He takes what is based upon truth and distorts it.

Wrong reliance on knowledge and power

The serpent tempted Eve with the suggestion that once she had eaten from the tree of knowledge she would be equal with God. In effect he was saying, 'Swallow this, and you won't have to rely on God any longer. You'll be able to call the shots for yourself.' Over the years that same temptation has been whispered to every one of us and, like Eve, all of us have at some time succumbed. The trouble is, we do not like to have to rely on God. We want to be able to manage for ourselves, and so often we think we can do a better job. The devil will do all in his power to foster this delusion and get us to rely on anything other than God.

A good example of this is medicine. Today medicine and medical techniques have reached such an advanced stage that it is all too easy for God to be left out of the picture entirely. Don't get me wrong—I believe medicine is a gift of God, but we can very easily get the balance wrong. A friend once told me that he was taking a short cut through the grounds of our local hospital on the way to the Post Office, when he bumped into two friends. A Christian couple, they had the misfortune of both having to receive treatment for serious, life-threatening conditions. They chatted for a while about the treatment they were undergoing, but at no point in the entire conversation, my friend said, was God mentioned, even though the couple professed to be Christians. Their faith was entirely in the doctors and the treatment they were receiving. Now I repeat that I am not trying to knock medicine here, but the devil does tempt us to put our trust in the things that are seen, and he finds it very easy to tempt us in the area of ill-health. All too often God is left out of the picture . . . and yet it is God who is the source of health and all healing.

The truth is actually both very simple and very complex. Anything that leads away from God and diverts our attention from him—causing us to give it 'worship'—is pleasing to the devil. This does not mean that we must reject things such as medicine, or learning in general, but it does mean that we must be careful to have the right attitude towards God, because the more precious the gift, the more the devil will seek to pervert it.

The devaluing of our humanity

The same principle lies at the heart of our personal relationships. Whatever is precious the devil will try to distort. Nowhere, for example, do we see this more clearly than in the area of sex. Sexual relations between a man and a woman are a gift of God, because they bind us more closely and underpin marriage. And yet, perhaps more than any other aspect of our lives, sex can become an area for sin. We see the deceptions of the devil at work in society today in the growing argument that 'anything goes'; that anything is right if it feels right to the individual and that, conversely, sin creeps in only when we object. But we can recognise that this is demonic, if for no other reason than the shattered and damaged lives resulting from people rejecting so-called traditional values and following these ideas.

Perversion of the truth that underlies our essential being is a very powerful temptation, and to give way to these kinds of enticement unquestionably opens us up to demonic hold. The first step, then, is to recognise what is going on for exactly what it is, and not to try to make excuses, either for ourselves or others. Once we recognise these lures as temptation, then (and only then) we can receive the grace to resist. But all too often these days, this kind of temptation can slip by without our even realising it is there, because as a society we have accepted the lie that sexual freedom means happiness, and that none of us has the right to judge the sexual practices of another.

Self-deception

It is a truth that God has only our best interests at heart, but sometimes there is a marked difference between our perception of our best interests and God's perception. We tend to think our interests are best served by the unruffled continuance of our comfort. God, however, does not always see it like this, especially if there is an area of wrong in our lives. This can apply equally both to our personal lives and to situations in which we may find ourselves involved.

There can be an enormous pressure to try to kid ourselves that something we or another has done wrong does not really matter, or even that God's interests will be best served by keeping quiet about something. Where this kind of situation arises, the devil will unquestionably get a hold unless and until both the attitude and area of wrong are repented of, and steps are taken to put the situation right.

I once came across a church where the vicar was all too clearly involved in an adulterous affair with a parishioner. His wife knew about it, the congregation knew about it, and the church authorities knew about it. He was indeed privately reprimanded by the bishop, but a decision was taken to try to subdue the affair, rather than attempt to address the situation publically and put matters right. One of the reasons given was that it would be damaging to the church if what had happened ever became known to the media. The church in question has since virtually collapsed.

We have already seen, in Joshua, the strange story of Achan, who brought military disaster upon the whole of Israel because, in direct disobedience to God, he kept back for himself some devoted objects taken from Jericho. We are told that Israel's sufferings were a direct consequence of their violation of the covenant—even though most of them were totally unaware of any such violation. But God said: 'I will not be with you any more unless you destroy whatever among you is devoted to destruction . . . You cannot stand against your enemies until you remove it' (Joshua 7:12–13).

Achan had listened to the whispers of temptation and deluded himself into believing that it would not matter if he helped himself to a couple of forbidden articles. But God knew that it would, and that if Achan was allowed to get away with this, the contagion would spread throughout Israel. Where there is an area of wrong, we delude ourselves when we succumb to the temptation to believe that it will not matter. We may even be trying to lead blameless lives, but where there is a wrong that we have not repented of, then the devil will unquestionably have a right of entry . . . and things will go wrong. They will go wrong because God will not be prepared to allow this double kind of allegiance.

Mistrust

A favourite form of demonic attack is the disruption of relationships and sowing of mistrust. The devil will do this in every way possible, whether by distorting reports of things said and done, or by playing on our own insecurities in a way that leads us to view others in a bad light. He especially likes to try to sow discord among Christians, and it is amazing how often, just when the Holy Spirit seems to be moving in real power, a major row erupts that leaves everyone reeling. Again, we should recognise this for what it is—temptation. We do no wrong until we succumb, and the way to counter this is by total openness and genuine love for others involved. As Christians we should all learn to avoid gossip, because that is a breeding ground for this kind of attack. Equally, where we become conscious of a dis-ease, we should in gentleness confront it, and not just hope that if we keep our heads down it will go away. It will not. The devil is very well aware of his success rate in this area.

Jealousy

Jealousy takes two forms. It is the emotion of mistrust that fears the betrayal (real or imagined) of another, which has its roots in insecurity. And it is the envy and fear of one whom we perceive as a rival, commonly coupled with an attempt to bring harm to that other. Jealousy, as we all know, is not simply confined to affairs of the heart, but pops up everywhere: in school, at work, in family relationships. Sadly, it all too often rears its head in church circles too. The devil is very quick to exploit this most primitive of human emotions and its underlying cause—the desire for worth.

What should we do? We can of course rebuke it in the name of the Lord. But where someone willingly entertains these feelings, they are not easily dealt with, especially since they are often tied to feelings of low self-worth and past pain . . . and jealousy can manifest in many different ways (it can even manifest as 'words from the Lord'). I would suggest that this situation needs to be met with great gentleness and love, but also, where appropriate, with honest (and still gentle) confrontation. If you are in a position where that is not possible (perhaps because you are in a subordinate position), then the right course of action is wholehearted compliance with any instructions—provided those instructions are not at variance with obedience to God. Where you recognise jealousy in yourself, then the first step is honest admission and repentance, coupled with a conscious attempt to act with tremendous consideration and love. Where mistrust is an element in a close relationship with another, then it may be good to ask someone you trust to pray with you for healing in areas of insecurity and then to share those feelings with the person concerned.

Anxiety and fear

God tells us to trust him for everything. The devil whispers to us that there is no security in life; that something terrible is going to happen, and that we are on our own. We have all met people who say they are 'born worriers'—we might even be such a person ourselves. But these feelings are not of God. Much is written today in books on spiritual warfare about rebuking such spirits, but I would like to suggest a rather different approach which focuses not on these feelings, but on God. We all face situations where we feel worry—it may be an exam, or a job interview; a loved one may be late coming home, and immediately we imagine something terrible and a police car pulling up outside. Or it may be a totally legitimate fear, in that someone we love is very ill, or we are very ill ourselves. I believe we all need to learn to be still with God and to allow his peace to come in. It is not that we actually want an absence of fear or anxiety. What we really want and need is the presence of peace, and it is only with God that we find this. If something upsets us, the first thing we should do is to bring it to God. Maybe at that point we hand over a whole heap of anxiety, and end up dissolving in tears. A lot of people do not like this (especially men!), but not only is that all right, it is very good—provided we then leave the problem with him.

I have lived long enough to discover that God never

fails us. We may find ourselves in a dire situation that is filled with intense pain, but God never lets us go and, amazingly, he can and does bring wonderful things out of the most terrible experiences, provided we let him. The devil will always try and whisper to us that 'this is it', but the thing to do is to ignore him, and a wonderful weapon here is praise. I know that sounds a strange thing to say to someone when they are at rock bottom and it is clearly the last thing they want to do, but it really does open up the way to God, and once we have allowed him in, we can trust him to sort out the situation.

I have always been struck by the story in Acts of Paul and Silas in prison in Philippi (16:23ff.). About midnight, we are told, they were praying and singing hymns to God. What a strange thing to do! Most of us in prison would be fairly depressed—we might even be a bit cross with God if we had found ourselves there because we were trying to do his work. Not Paul and Silas though, because they knew that the way to counter fear and anxiety was with praise. It would be all right, because God would look after them! And in fact this is the real healing for uncontrollable feelings of anxiety: the absolute knowledge, because we have been there before, that God cannot and will not fail us when the chips are down. Paul and Silas knew that what they had to do in this situation was not to rebuke spirits of hardness on the part of the magistrates, or spirits of unbelief or whatever. No, what they had to do was praise, and sure enough, God responded (and in a totally unexpected way). First there was an earthquake and all their chains fell off . . . and then the gaoler was converted! When you think about it, it was a pretty effective antidote to fear.

A point that should also be made in this section is that many Christians complain of spiritual attack when they first become actively involved in work for God. This is an interesting and very real phenomenon—and the effects are far too powerful to be dismissed as mere by-products of the imagination. The first thing to understand is that the devil will move every time he sees work in hand that is going to add to the glory of the King. He wants that glory, so he is going to try to spoil it—he did it with Jesus, so there is no reason we should be exempt. The more committed we are to God's work, the high probability is that the more powerfully, and more constantly, we shall be attacked. But this is by no means as dire as it sounds, because where this is the case, God helps. It is actually perfectly possible to be suffering under the most devastating attack and yet to be totally at peace; and, moreover, to be experiencing real joy. At the same time, what God tends to do is to expose our areas of weakness through these attacks, and especially any deficiencies in our relationship with himself. The answer, where we feel disturbance of spirit, is to spend more time alone with him. This is not to say that we shall not feel real pain in situations of difficulty, and we know that all of the prophets and even Jesus himself (eg, Mark 15:34) had their low spots. But that pain will not bind us, and it will be totally unable to separate us from God.

In all things, then, God is sovereign, and in whatever way the devil attacks, it can ultimately work only for our good. The complete answer in any situation, as said above, is to come to a point of stillness before God—because it is there that God will meet with us and respond. So when things go wrong, the first thing to do is say, 'Thank you, God, that you are sovereign here.

What are you trying to teach me?' We need in all things to be still, and to trust ourselves to God's love. Where there is anxiety, ask for the gift of trust.

The myth of tolerance

This is one of the most effective weapons in the devil's armoury of temptation today. I think there must have been tremendous rejoicing in the nether regions when one of the demons came up with this one, and here in Britain we are particularly vulnerable, because we all pride ourselves so terribly on 'fair play' and 'letting the other chap have his say'. It is the myth that we must not interfere with the freedoms of another because that will cause harm. Again, the devil has taken a basic core of God-given truth and totally distorted it. And it attacks every area of life.

We must no longer, for example, insist on the uniqueness of Christ because that is insulting to people of other faiths. And we must ignore the fact not only that they may well lay claims to exclusive revelation themselves, but also that they may well be intent on asserting those claims with both violence and aggression, while they have not the slightest intention of extending a similar tolerance to ourselves. We must not say that we believe certain sexual practices are wrong, because that is judgemental, and people with those predelictions have a right to follow whatever way seems good to them. We must respect the religious beliefs and moral codes of others, but we must not expect similar consideration ourselves. This last was illustrated all too clearly in the controversy over the film *The Last Temptation of Christ*. It was apparently seen by many as wholly acceptable that Jesus Christ should be portrayed in a way that Christians found offensive. But a Muslim protest over the use of a verse from the Koran (which was not obviously insulting) on a dress designed by Chanel for the 1994 fashion shows was met by total and immediate capitulation, and everybody found their feelings of outrage totally understandable.

Now I am not saying that we should as a society insult people of other faiths. I am merely pointing out how very intolerant this socially vociferous tolerance often is when it comes to all things Christian, and that it is a temptation which we must resist, however unpopular we may become with those who do not share our faith. It is not that we must resist in a spirit of condemnation (which the devil, I suspect, would find as acceptable as our meek compliance), but that we really must stand for our beliefs, because anything less than that is dishonouring to God.

'Signaphilia'

Another area in which I believe the devil is very active today is in the reliance on experience and constant seeking after signs which, in at least some sections of the church, seems almost to have reached epidemic proportions. Now it is entirely right that we should seek the Lord's will for our lives, but some Christians today appear to be totally incapable of making even the most minor decision without some direct guidance from God. I do not believe that this is the way God wants us to live. We do not need divine guidance over whether or not to have an egg or cereal for breakfast. God is completely capable of revealing his will to us if he wants, and he is also capable of leading us in a certain direction, or even preventing us from embarking on a course of action if it is not what he wants, so I really do believe that the right thing to do is simply to submit everything to God, and unless he chooses to reveal something, we just carry on. We must not seek after signs.

I have come across people today, however, who not only seek after signs in respect of their own lives, but also for everyone with whom they come into contact. These are the people to whom God 'speaks' every morning. They regularly see visions or have experiences, and they are constantly receiving 'words of knowledge' giving insight into the lives of others. I am sure I am not alone when I say that I regularly have people coming to me with 'words of knowledge' about my life. The Lord has told them to tell me that I have to do such-and-such, or go somewhere, or not go somewhere, or that there is some area of deep bondage from which he wishes to release me. Now I am sure that there are deep bondages from which the Lord wishes to release me, and equally I am convinced that he does have plans for my life, but although there are occasions when God does speak to us through others, on the whole I have learned to trust myself to him. My usual response now when people say this kind of thing to me is that if it really were from the Lord, I would have expected him to give me some sort of indication too. Without that, I ignore it.

I believe this seeking after signs is not only wrong and offensive to God, but can also cause terrible damage. The proper thing to do is to seek *nothing* and, if one does have any kind of revelation or experience, *ignore it*. No, this is not blasphemy. If it really is from God you will not be able to shut it out; and if it is a word of revelation about the future for yourself, you do not actually need to do anything, because if God says he will do something, then *he* will bring it about. Therefore crucify experience, so that anything that is not of God can be burned away. Turn it out and say to God, 'If it is of you, Lord, then confirm this independently, please.' God will not be angry, because the devil can all too easily pose as an angel of light, and he will happily feed us all sorts of experiences if it results in our becoming focused away from God. Satan can even sometimes give us some very 'religious' experiences, but it does not make them good!

I am actually one of the last people to deny that God does speak to and guide us. Indeed, I believe that the closer we get to God, the more powerfully aware we become of his guidance, both for ourselves and others. But there is a world of difference between consciously seeking after signs and consciously seeking only after God. The first is magic, and delights the devil. The second is faith, and terrifies him. The charismatic wing of the church has done wonders in recalling people to a living and dynamic relationship with God, empowered by the Holy Spirit, but the constant emphasis on experience, and the formulae that have emerged, are a menace! We must beware getting caught by religiosity and the supernatural, and giving worship not to God, but to lesser gods posing as angels of light.

13
Come Close to God

The ways of temptation are many and devious, and it is not my intention in this book to try to list every possible variation, but simply to demonstrate some of the key areas in which we are attacked. The devil will always try to attack us, and the complete answer is always to stay close to God, and be absolutely obedient to everything he says. We are going to fail of course, but God is not asking us to be perfect before we get to know him. What he is asking of us is that we commit ourselves to him, and try. He will do the rest. That means we have to be very careful to obey. But there is, of course, another scenario here which has to be addressed, and that is: What do we do when it is clear that the devil has got a hold? It is one thing to resist, but what if it is apparent someone or something (and it might even be ourselves) has fallen, and the very idea of resisting appears to be too late?

The complete answer for every one of us is to come closer to God, and the same principles actually hold good. For example, if you find yourself in a situation where it feels that things are seriously wrong, in the first instance simply ask God for help. Now it may be that he will lead you to rebuke something (because rebuking does seem to be rather fashionable these days). But that is by no means inevitable, and the proper course first of all is to come against whatever is there in an opposing spirit. I well remember being told of a church a couple of years back, where the eldership felt, over time, that God was revealing to them a spirit of greed. They felt it was revealed to them that this spirit was dominating everything they did (and I must say, the more one thought about it, it really did seem right). What to do? They could of course have told it to go away, but what they actually felt God saying to them was: 'Give—and give without ceasing.' Not surprisingly, this was something they found extremely difficult, but they obeyed, and the result is now a thriving and dynamic church. But it was only through this incredibly 'sacrificial giving' that their greed was put to flight. This is an opposing spirit or attitude.

The same principle holds good for every situation in which we might find ourselves. For example, you might be part of a group where suddenly everyone starts criticising you, and not just a few gentle and helpful remarks, but a real attempt to try and take you apart! In this situation the temptation is enormous to let rip and retaliate in kind, but actually this is not helpful. To give way to this will only make things far worse. The only helpful course you can take is first commit the whole situation to God and ask him to sort it out, and then go back into the situation in the opposing spirit, which means in forgiveness and gentleness, and with a total refusal to respond in kind.

Nonetheless, it remains sadly true that there are some troubled souls for whom all hell seems to break loose whenever they try to come closer to God. In my experience, this is because there is an area in their lives over which the devil has control. It may be as a result of something they have themselves done, in which case it needs repentance and release. It may be something done to them, in which case they need to forgive and ask for healing and release. Or it may be something in which they themselves have not been actively involved at all, as sometimes happens in the case of generational sin.

These are all real problems, and where they occur, they must not be dismissed as just 'all in the mind'. Very often, simply counselling someone on how to cope in these kinds of situation is not going to provide an answer. These are people who are badly spiritually hurt, and what they most need, in order to be healed, is to be set free.

The kind of scenarios I have in mind are where, for example, someone actually starts to fight where there is prayer taking place, or reacts with extreme terror, even though they may themselves have been the one to ask for prayer. Or someone may complain of a constant babble of voices inside their head, which are making all sorts of unpleasant and outrageous suggestions. Or they may not be able to control their behaviour, whether it is a repetitive behavioural response or an extreme reaction in certain circumstances. I do not propose to enter into a lengthy section on deliverance here, but simply to point out that God *is* sovereign, and before him the devil cannot maintain a hold. Beyond that, I believe that these things call for a definite area of gifting and I would simply want to encourage people to seek help. I would also caution people who have not been led very clearly into this ministry by God, not to dive in and start rebuking everything in sight, on the theory that at some point they are going to strike home. I have seen people enormously helped and blessed by this form of ministry, but I have also come across people who have been very badly damaged too. God wants his children set free; he does not want them maimed.

Of course, it is not always clear until after you have started praying with someone that this kind of problem is present—and I well remember asking the Lord's blessing for someone after a service one Sunday and they went down, and appeared to be engaged in some form of shadow wrestling. At this point, it became clear that something very untoward was going on. My advice in this situation would be to seal whatever it is with the blood of the Lamb and forbid it in Jesus' name to cause any further harm until the Lord deals with it . . . and then go and get help!

It may even be that as you read this you have a real fear that this is you who is being described, because (bizarre as it may sound) there are many Christians around today who are really worried that they might be possessed. Do not be afraid. Trust God.

Yet again, we see two extremes of reaction here: on the one hand, stark terror which leads some to reject completely the idea that a Christian can be possessed; and, on the other, a positive orgy of trying to identify demons at work, both personally and in others. Both attitudes, I believe, are extremely dangerous and are actually giving worship to the devil. As I have tried to show, all of us carry the effects of hurts and sins, and some of these effects unquestionably bring about bondage in our lives. We all have these kinds of problems—it is a part of the human condition—and a major work of the Holy Spirit is actually to bring about our gradual healing and release—to make us *Christ-like*.

It may be that there is a very obvious bondage affecting us—one that shows up, for example, as chronic depression, or something like an inability to form relationships. The permutations are endless, and we only need to look at our own lives to discover a few! Sometimes there can be a situation where we know there is a problem—we can see it, we know what we are doing wrong, but try as we might, we just cannot break it, and it's as though every time we try, there is an iron band that comes down on us and cripples us! Christians are as liable to this as any other member of the human race. The difference is, we know that Christ frees.

Sometimes, however, that process of freeing can take quite a while—we might indeed feel bound up and oppressed for years! Such feelings do not mean that nothing is going on. Indeed, throughout this time we can have absolute assurance that the Holy Spirit is working extremely hard, and that what he is doing is getting us to a point of complete release. The odd thing is that the closer we get, the more horrendous everything can become—we can even feel that we are totally falling apart. Hard as this can be to accept, this is not something to fear—it is merely the drawing up of all that has been hurting us to the surface; a little bit like the ripening of a boil. Sometimes we need to ask someone to pray for us as God brings us to this point, but equally sometimes not—there really is no magic formula. When, however, that boil is lanced (and it must be lanced by God), it can sometimes feel like a really explosive release; and when that happens, something that has had a grip really goes.

Now is this a demon? It is most certainly something demonic that has had a wrong hold on our lives and that has been hurting us. But I do not believe that it means we have been 'possessed'. Demonic possession comes from invitation and is something very different indeed. We open ourselves up to demonic hold by wrong 'choices'; but we open ourselves up to possession by invitation, which may or may not have been conscious. For example, someone who becomes involved in white magic is issuing a wide-open invitation to the devil. They may not think they are, but without a doubt the devil sees things rather differently, and where someone has been involved in activities of this nature, if and when they become a Christian, they will need to be cut free. The same applies to any form of cultic or quasi-magical involvement. Freedom comes through confessing and repenting before Christ, and telling whatever it is to go in the name of the Lord, before asking Christ himself to come in and effect release. There needs to be a definite and clear change of sovereignty.

If this is you, as you read this book, and you are aware of an area of your life where you have given worship to 'another god', then please go and ask someone of spiritual maturity to pray with you. *Remember that Christ is sovereign*, and that it is actually his battle. The good news is, he has already won. Again, do not be afraid. God loves you.

Long ago, writing to the churches at Galatia, the Apostle Paul wrote: 'I have been crucified with Christ and I no longer live, but Christ lives in me' (Galatians 2:20). Therein lies our complete freedom. Possession comes about through the giving of allegiance to the one whose will is to destroy; oppression comes through the hold enabled by unrepented sin. Both are dealt with by Christ.

Wherever there is unrepented sin in our lives, that means we have denied Christ access. In effect, we have said, 'No, Lord, you can't have that area.' This means that the devil has a hold over us through this area. It's not sealed by the blood of the Lamb, he thinks, so he can come in. This hold is unquestionably demonic. We have refused to allow Jesus to come into that area so that he can take the sin and block Satan's access, and so forces hostile to God (demons) are quick to move in. In a very real sense these forces then begin to harry and oppress the believer, hoping in this way to extend their control and, in time, take possession. It is at this point, as we have already seen, that battle is joined. It is the work of the Spirit to protect and teach us, and one of the main things he will be trying to do throughout this struggle is to get us to the point of telling Jesus about this problem area and giving it to him totally—so that he can come in and deal with any demonic influences there are direct. Demonic hold is broken by confession and repentance. Our sincere repentance crucifies the sin, which Christ then takes wholly and completely. In return, he clothes us with his righteousness. The devil and his hoardes have no hold over Christ, and so we are set free.

Problems arise where, having confessed and repented of a particular sin, we then try and seize it back or refuse to let go: it is a little bit like Lazarus being called forth from the tomb, and refusing to come out. Or like a drowning man fighting with his rescuer, because he does not trust him to get him safely to shore. Christians in this situation need to realise fully the freedom that is held out to them by Christ. They need to discover the reality of crucifixion for themselves, because the death of self is actually our freedom and perfect defence (Matthew 10:38–39).

The devil only has access with permission, and if we will allow Jesus to stand in the gaping hole of our sin, that access is denied. But repentance means obedience and conversion of life. It means the total giving of our allegiance to the King—and then we come under the King's protection and rule. More than anything else the devil and his minions fear this. It is so simple and can sometimes seem so hard, but actually all it is, is letting go. Oppression is broken by repentance.

Epilogue

Throughout this book I have tried to show where our understanding of the nature of evil comes from, and precisely what that means for us today. The devil is not some equal and opposed force to God, but neither is he a figment of our overworked imaginations. God is sovereign, although the devil would like to con us into believing that he is not even there at all! The devil does not mind if we do not expressly worship him. What he does want is that we do not worship God, and anything that gets in the way of that he actually counts as victory to himself. More than that, anything which gets in the way he sees as worship of himself, because it separates us from God and binds us more securely to himself. The devil is quite happy to hide behind the image of ourselves, our jobs, our hatreds, our worldly goods . . . even our religion.

But he cannot win, and he has in fact already been defeated. No matter how hard he has worked to try to deceive and destroy us, there *is* only one God, and the amazing thing is that this sovereign Lord, whose power is unimaginable, loves us. More than that, he fights on our behalf.

This world is a battleground, but the real place of

battle is not actually here in the material, but takes place in heaven. It is the spirit that matters, and more than anything else, it is our relationship with God that releases us into life and real joy. The devil is the ancient foe of men and women, but he is, and always has been, inferior to God. Within the world, we are subject to his onslaught, but our freedom lies in God. When we stand in the shadow at God's side, then we are assured of his protection and, more than that, of victory. In our sinfulness and our weakness, it is foolish to focus on someone who is decidedly inferior to God. God is the only one we should fear.

Scripture Index

Genesis
1:2ff. 242
1:6–7 160
1:26ff. 193
1:28 90
1:31 81
2:7 156
2:16–17 32
3:1 35, 81
3:7 41
3:14–15 82
3:22 41
3:22–24 40
3:24 196, 227
5:22–24 179
6 187, 204
6:4 160
6:5 48
11:5 44
11:6–7 45
11:19 44
16:13–14 180
19 184, 186
19:1–29 224
19:4–9 48
21:17 183
32:30 179
37:2–11 63
37:23f. 63
39:3 63
39:13–20 64
39:21 64

Exodus
3:6 180
3:13 21
20:4–6 230
20:8–10 55

Leviticus
17:7 209
26:3–9 52

Numbers
1:50–51 57
22 241
22:6 242
22:21–35 186
25:1–9 49

Deuteronomy

6:16	130
8:5	66
8:19–20	49
18:10–12	158
18:20	158
28	231
28:20	231
32:8	217
32:17	210

Joshua

6	49
7:12	50
7:12–13	258

Judges

4:1	95
6:1	95
10:6	95

1 Samuel

10	54
10:9–11	99
10:9–13	240
15:10–23	99
16:14f.	100
16:23–24	100
18:10–12	53
31:1–6	100

2 Samuel

5–6	56
6:1ff.	56
24:1	96
24:15–17	184
24:17	103

1 Kings

18	95
19:5–7	183
20:28	229
22:1–18	100
22:19–23	181
22:22–23	183
22:23	101

2 Kings

1:3–4	183
3:26–27	161
16:3–4	161
19:35–36	183

1 Chronicles

21:1	96
21:7ff.	216

2 Chronicles

3:7–14	196
18:1–27	100

Job

1–2	103
1:6	95, 180
1:9–12	186
1:11	27
2:1f.	180
2:4–5	27
6	152
10:21	158
38:4–7	181

Psalms

16:10	159
18:4	158
49:13–14	158
74:13–14	160
81:13–14	219
86:13	158
88:12	158
89:7	180
91:11–12	129
91:13	85
94:17	158
103:2–3	157
109:6	97
139:8	159

Proverbs

9:10	184

Isaiah

3:16–26	46
6:2	195
14	220
14:12	117
14:12–15	88, 164
14:13–14	109
22:8–25	46
24:21–22	160
27:1	84
55:8f.	180

Jeremiah

7:18–31	162
7:31	162
31:29	71

Ezekiel

10	196
10:9–17	192
18:2	71
18:3–24	71
28:11–19	89
28:12–19	109
37:7–10	156
32:14	159

Daniel

7:22	183
10:4–14	217
10:10–14	194
10:12–13	218
10:20–21	218
12	224
12:1f.	220

Amos

1–4	229
3:6	97

Haggai

2:12–13	27

Zechariah

3	227
3:1	97
3:1–2	181

Matthew

2:16–18	111
4:1	142
4:1–11	120, 127
4:3	147

4:10	143
4:11	185
4:17	109
5:22	162
7:16	101
8:28–34	120
10:28	162
10:38–39	274
12:1–14	117
12:22–26	144
12:24	130
12:28	145
12:39f.	130
13:19	147
13:24f.	135
16:13–16	131
16:21–23	127
18:10	207
22:23–33	170
24:1–51	121, 164
26:59–61	134
26:61	136
27:40	127

Mark

1:12–13	120, 127
1:13	142
1:14–15	109
2:23–28	117
3:21	131
3:22	130
3:23–27	144
5:6–20	125
8:27–30	131
8:33	132
9:43ff.	162
9:43–44	163
12:18–27	170
13	164
13:1–37	121
13:10ff.	248
15:34	262

Luke

1:26	183
2:30–32	119
4:1	142
4:1–13	120, 127
4:18–19	116
4:18–21	109
4:33–35	124
4:34	119
4:40–41	119
4:41f.	124
6:1–11	116–117
6:5	55
8:26–33	163
8:28	138
9:18–20	131
10:18	91, 117
11:15	130
11:17–22	144
11:21–22	137, 139
12:5	162
13:1–5	118
16:19–31	167
16:25–26	163
17:1	114
20:27–38	170
21:5–36	121, 164
22:31–32	224
22:41–44	140

John

1:1f.	242
1:1–3	181
1:1–5	108
1:10–12	108
1:32–34	116
2:19–21	136
3:1–10	132
5:14	118
8:3-11	117
8:12	145
8:44	147, 247
12:31	145
14:29–31	118
14:30	117, 140, 145
16:11	145
18:36	145
19:11	60

Acts

5:1–10	58
12:7–10	183
12:21–32	47
13:7–11	47
16:16	158
16:23ff.	261
18:1–2	228
19:28	215
20:29–31a	14
23:8–9	201

Romans

1:18ff.	135
1:24–32	53
7:18–19	22
8:28	182
8:38–39	223
13:1	192, 221

1 Corinthians

6:3	193
10:13	38
10:16	241
10:19f.	144
10:19–21	210
11:10	187
11:27–30	17
11:27–32	241

2 Corinthians

11:3	147
11:14	147

Galatians

2:20	272
3:13	232
5:21	169

Ephesians

2:2	146

Colossians

1:15–16	223
2:18f.	189

2 Thessalonians

2:3–4	172
2:9–10	172

Hebrews

1:14	214

2:18	38	20:7f.	167
13:2	186	20:7–15	115
		20:10	167
James		20:13	167
1:13–14	31	20:14	167
3:8	243		
4:7	211, 236	*Apocrypha and Pseudepigrapha*	

1 John
2:18–23	172

2 Esdras
7:36	162

Jude
9	9

Tobit
8:2–3	185
12:12–15	186

Revelation
1:5	140
9:1	164
10ff.	172
11:7	172
12:4	220
12:7	152
12:9	84
13:4–8	173
16:13	201
19:20	167
20:2	84
20:4ff.	168

Ecclesiasticus
17:17	217

Enoch
18:12–16	161
40:1–10	187
88:1	161

Ascension of Moses
10:6	160